Revealing Essays that Will Change
the Way You Think About Age

MIDLIFE
PRIVATE
PARTS

EDITED BY
DINA ALVAREZ & DINA ARONSON

A REGALO PRESS BOOK
ISBN: 979-8-88845-934-8
ISBN (eBook): 979-8-88845-935-5

Midlife Private Parts:
Revealing Essays that Will Change the Way You Think About Age
© 2025 by Off Script Media, LLC
All Rights Reserved

Cover Design by Jim Villaflores

Publishing Team:
Founder and Publisher – Gretchen Young
Acquiring Editor – Debra Englander
Editorial Assistant – Caitlyn Limbaugh
Managing Editor – Caitlin Burdette
Production Manager – Kate Harris
Production Editor – Courtney Michaelson

As part of the mission of Regalo Press, a donation is being made to Let's Talk Menopause as chosen by the author. Find out more about this organization at https://www.letstalkmenopause.org/.

This book, as well as any other Regalo Press publications, may be purchased in bulk quantities at a special discounted rate. Contact orders@regalopress.com for more information.

This is a work of nonfiction. All people, locations, events, and situations are portrayed to the best of the author's memory.

Regalo Press
New York • Nashville
regalopress.com

Published in the United States of America
1 2 3 4 5 6 7 8 9 10

*To my mother, who remains very much alive in
my heart, and whose grace, strength, courage, and
resilience continue to inspire me from beyond.*
—Dina Aronson

*To all the women in my family, my ancestral guides, who steer
me when I can't find my way. To my mother, for stepping on
that plane in 1966 and giving me the chance of a better life.*
—Dina Alvarez

For age is opportunity no less
Than youth itself, though in another dress,
And as the evening twilight fades away
The sky is filled with stars, invisible by day.
—Henry Wadsworth Longfellow

*I don't believe in aging. I believe in forever altering
one's aspect to the sun. Hence my optimism.*
—Virginia Woolf

There are some things you learn best in calm, and some in storm.
—Willa Cather

I dwell in Possibility.
—Emily Dickinson

Table of Contents

Chapter 10
Style for the Ages: Dress to Impress (Yourself)

Chapter 11
Notes on Invisibility: Can You See Me Now?

Chapter 12
The Last Place I Ever Thought I'd Be

Introduction

Enter the phrase "midlife women" into any search engine, and you might think that we're all destined to fall off a cliff once we hit a certain age. Article after article on the "midlife crisis" details the existential angst; the loss of youth, beauty, and identity, the burnout, and the feelings of despair that there is more in the rearview than lies ahead. Per Google, being a midlife woman can be a pretty bleak state of affairs.

But this is not your mother's middle age, and fortunately, the cultural conversation around aging has started to shift. We are finally (and mercifully) talking about topics like menopause, which until recently seemed to be the last of the great taboos in this country, and we are slowly chipping away at outdated notions around age and showing by example that, as George Eliot once said, "It's never too late to be what you might have been."

Still, being a midlife woman today can feel very lonely. Many of us are emerging from a world in which our roles and identities up to this point were tied to others—mother, wife, daughter, colleague, and so on. We are now transitioning to a new chapter, and it can feel much different from the life we have known. So many of us have spent our earlier years doing what we thought we "should" do, uncomfortably contorting ourselves to fit into spaces that we have now outgrown. But where *do* we fit? Some days it can feel as though the rug has been pulled out from under us.

Facing the question "What's next?" can feel daunting, especially at 4 a.m. on yet another sweaty, sleepless night. And as we try to answer these big, consequential questions, many of us are hit with a host of unexpected emotions that come with the territory but can leave us wondering if we are losing our minds. One minute we are going about our lives, the next we are sobbing in the grocery store parking lot. Then there's the ten minutes we spent searching for the glasses that were right on top of our head, or the hundreds of things we *actually* misplaced, or the entirely generic word that we can't recall to save our lives. The list of things that can make us feel unhinged goes on and on.

And that's why we felt compelled to bring this book into being. Because if you're reading it, surely you have days when you are wondering what the hell is going on. We all have them, and we want you to know you are "normal," even when your life starts to feel anything but. We wanted to share real stories from real women, not in whispers, but in big, bold, amplified shouts. In these pages you will see yourself, and if you are feeling lost, you will find yourself. You will recognize your rage and your desires; you will feel familiar reckonings with your past, and you will see your struggles and triumphs reflected in these powerful, poignant stories. Most importantly, in reading these pages, you will feel connected to a big and beautiful sisterhood—one that sees, hears, and understands you.

Told through the eyes of contemporary women, including writers, authors, and creatives, each shares a story of coming to terms with aging and the unexpected moments that define midlife while also embracing and redefining who they have become.

In their stories, their struggles, and their triumphs, you will find connection, validation, and—we promise—inspiration.

Whether it's menopause or sexual pleasure, midlife reinvention, friendship, redefining style at a certain age, dating after divorce, feeling invisible, or simply being in the last place they ever thought they would be, each essay embodies a midlife moment; a revelation and new hope for the future. The stories they tell reveal who they've become through the experience of meeting midlife head on rather than fading into the background.

We've intentionally chosen a diverse group of women to share their stories; some are career writers, and others have come to writing more recently; some have reinvented themselves as podcasters, designers, and midlife educators; others have taken bold steps to become entrepreneurs and market disruptors. And for good measure, we threw in a rock star menopause doctor. You will not find perfect symmetry here—like life, this book unfolded in ways both beautiful and unexpected. At its center there is great heart, and we decided to let it beat.

The beauty of anthologies is that the reader can pick up anywhere; unlike a novel, every essay is an opportunity to start anew with a fresh perspective always at your fingertips. Whether you choose to jump around or devour in order, we know that these stories will resonate and empower you to see this time as one of great possibilities. Because the truth is that when we reframe the way we think about age, midlife can be an amazing opportunity to reimagine life, find new meaning and purpose, and live more intentionally and more boldly than ever.

CHAPTER 1

Shifting Identities

Getting Older and Bolder

When I let go of what I am, I become what I might be.
—Lao Tzu

Not Without My Readers

JESSICA FEIN

The summer before I started high school, I decided to upgrade my look. I swapped my stack of Izod shirts for peasant blouses, my Jordache jeans for long flowy skirts. I stopped feathering my hair and started wearing it curly. The change I was most excited about was replacing my glasses with contact lenses.

Now, some forty years later, I still wear contacts, but I supplement them with the dozen pairs of glasses I keep scattered around my house. I have glasses for reading and glasses for glare, another set for distance and several for the sun. It's not only that I can easily spend twenty minutes looking for my glasses when they're on top of my head, it's also that I have better night vision when I'm wearing distance glasses on top of my reading glasses. It's a special look, to be sure, but what it lacks in form it makes up for ten times over in function.

I see things differently now. And not just in the literal sense.

My teens and twenties were about shaping my perspectives as I figured out who I wanted to be and how I wanted to show up in the world. In my thirties and early forties, I wore my views proudly, confident they fit me perfectly. But now it seems I'm looking at big things and small in entirely new ways.

I even see myself differently.

Case in point: For most of my life, I prided myself on being a problem solver. It didn't matter what the challenge was, I'd be the one to come up with the solution…and do it quickly.

My gift for problem-solving probably started in second grade on the day I got a perfect score *and* was the first one in class to finish the math worksheet. I got not one, but two gold stars on my paper. That was all the confirmation I needed to understand that gold stars come to those who know the answers and don't dillydally in making them known.

From then on I was an answer seeker. Over time the challenges went from speed rounds in math to filling blue books front to back to helping people I love figure out which job to choose, which house, which partner. Solution mode was my comfort zone.

But then my sister was diagnosed with stage 4 lung cancer. "We got this," I promised her as I pored over medical reports I didn't understand and made spreadsheets comparing clinical trials around the world. "If we need to, we'll find a cure in the rainforests of Cambodia," I promised, having no idea whether there were rainforests in Cambodia and, if there were, why they'd be harboring a cure for cancer.

One night after yet another scary scan, I was trying desperately to cheer her up. I may as well have been waving pom-poms in the air when she stopped me and quietly said, "Jess, please don't try to problem solve right now. I just need you to be with me in my fear and sadness."

I dropped my pom poms and wrapped my arms around her. And I realized I'd never once asked my sister what she wanted or needed from me.

That's when I learned that it's not really about finding all the answers. It's about asking the right questions. It's not that

I didn't care about how other people felt before; it's just that I thought I already knew how they felt, what they needed.

There I was in bona fide middle age, a time when I might have taken pride in being set in my hard-earned ways. Instead I was shifting my view.

If that had been it, I might have assumed *this* midlife change, the one I wasn't expecting, was an exception. But there was more.

I used to think making a difference meant doing something on a grand scale. I grew up in a home where the idea of *tikkun olam*—the Jewish concept of mending the world—was dinner-table conversation. What I really wanted to talk about was tryouts for the lacrosse team or why my friends Liz and Dana were ganging up on me. Meanwhile my parents were reminding me that "ours is not to complete the task, nor are we free to desist from it."

Really?

I didn't even know what the task was. Surely they weren't thinking about loading the dishwasher or finishing my homework.

My father told me more than once that my inheritance was being born to a family of "carers," people who were preoccupied with making the world a better place. My problem with his charge was that the world is a very big place, and it seemed an unrealistically tall order.

When I graduated from college I did as expected, working first at a nonprofit in DC and then at one in Seattle. My turn to writing and then marketing coincided with my lengthy journey to becoming a mother. By then I'd given up on changing the world and was looking merely to change my own life.

It took almost a decade, but I finally became a mom—three times over—when my husband and I adopted our brood from Guatemala. Now it was time to turn inward to my kids. Forget about fixing the world, there was laundry to do and baths to draw and meals to make. The kitchen itself needed a lot of tikkun-ing.

As my kids got older, they required even more of my time. Our middle child had a rare, degenerative disease, and our eldest had ADHD with a host of accompanying emotional and learning issues. My dad suggested I join this advocacy organization and that support group.

"I'm way too focused on my trees," I told him. "I just don't care about the forest right now."

Night after night I read aloud with my eldest. Picture books became chapter books and then textbooks. "We'll get through this together," I said, when the assignments became more complicated than anything I'd learned in school, and we both struggled. Meanwhile, my husband and I titrated meds and held our daughter's trembling hand as she faced her illness head on, and it grew increasingly more debilitating. We did everything we could to help our children be kind and happy people even as their challenges increased.

I watered my trees and gave them light and nurtured them in every possible way. I watched my sisters and my friends and the other medical mamas I met along the way doing the same with their kids, and I realized that all these trees taken together make one hell of a forest.

Now I know that changing the world doesn't have to look big. The small moments, one after the other, can make the world a better place too.

I guess it's not surprising that I'm changing my mind about so many things these days. Everything else about my body is changing—my belly, my skin, my hair—why not my mind too?

And speaking about my body, from age ten to fifty I refused to be seen in a bathing suit that didn't have shorts and/or a skirt built in. God forbid a touch of tushy peeked out of the bathing suit bottom. My friends wore string bikinis. Meanwhile I could have gone straight from the beach to high-holiday services without changing. At least I was prepared.

Now I wear whatever bathing suit I like, with little concern for what's peeking out, or even hanging out. The irony is that I wish I'd flaunted the body I had even five years ago. These days, I know my body of today will look fabulous to the me of tomorrow, so I'm dressing accordingly. Besides, I've finally begun to believe the trope that the most attractive thing you can wear is confidence.

I've changed my mind about naps, which I'm now in favor of, and tequila too. I no longer think sneakers are just for exercise or that vacations where there's nothing to do are boring.

I'd always imagined that by the time I was half a century old, I'd be stalled in my tracks, unapologetic about the beliefs and habits I'd developed over time. I didn't think I'd be interested in changing, or even willing to. I thought the years of exploration would expire, and I'd be tucked under a cozy throw on the living room couch, eating, drinking, and thinking the same things in perpetuity.

Instead, I've surprised myself. I'm in somewhat of a renaissance period where it feels as though everything's up for grabs. I recently left the corporate job I held for twenty-five years. I launched my own podcast. I'm writing more, and sometimes, on days when I feel particularly bold, I'll dare to call myself "a writer." I'm even looking at real estate listings on the coast opposite from where I've lived my whole life.

Perhaps it's because I no longer care what others think of my choices. I'm not trying to please my parents or climb a career ladder or attract a new partner. (The partner I have, by the way, is perfectly delighted with my updated beach look.) I've lived with myself long enough to know who I am *and* be excited about who I might become.

I'm not sure how I'll see things on the journey ahead, but I do know that I'll keep moving forward and I'll keep changing. I also know this: I plan to be packing an assortment of glasses for all of it.

When You're No Longer the New Kid on the Block

JULIE FLAKSTAD

I found myself crying twice that week, looking out my bedroom window.

Maybe it was the upcoming holiday season stirring up emotions, or the financial stress of our kitchen renovation gone awry, or the combination of a new fifty-pound puppy on top of our already prickly, hormonal teenagers that had me twisted inside out. The unsteadiness of it all made me feel fragile. Or maybe it was the message that Nancy had left weeks earlier about their move and the parade of moving vans now parked across the street. It suddenly felt overwhelming.

In her somewhat thin, whispery voice, Nancy had left a voicemail explaining that she and her husband Bill were putting their house on the market. They were moving. She wanted to let me know so that we weren't alarmed by the unusual number of cars parked outside. They were very neighborly that way; they liked everything just so, including their hedges, which Nancy neatly trimmed every week. It made sense; I had noticed Bill looking increasingly frail, but even so, there was an impending gravity to it. It felt like a changing of the guard.

DINA ALVAREZ & DINA ARONSON

We had met Bill and Nancy Goodwin almost fourteen years earlier when we traded our New York City rental for a suburban life with convenient public schools and a backyard. My son, two and a half at the time, in his tiny easy-on-easy-off jeans with the elastic waistband, racing toward the bathroom hoping he'd make it in time, and my daughter, just a year old, wobbling around in the snow, her pink woolen skullcap covering her entire head, neck, and little chin. Bill and Nancy were the first ones to welcome us to our new neighborhood. They lived alone, their children grown up, and although they were a bit formal, like many of their generation, there was a mutual, unspoken understanding that if we ever needed anything, they were just across the street.

As our kids grew up, we settled in—dinner parties, after-noon playdates, back-to-school nights, and endless weekend sports. It was our own little galaxy—us orbiting our children, their friends, and the families that surrounded them—but we waved to Bill and Nancy in between the hustle and bustle, exchanged the occasional phone call, and kept an eye on their house when they eventually began wintering in Florida. Bill loved golf. Years later when our kids were in junior high school, we saw them one day at church. "We're not going to Florida anymore," Nancy confided in me softly during coffee hour. "We need to be closer to church," she said, looking over at Bill, who seemed distant at best. I couldn't help but wish that Bill could have both.

Bill and Nancy's house sold in four days. They accepted an offer from a young family in town while another couple was mid-flight on their way from California hoping to see it. I got the scoop from a different neighbor who had heard the full story via their realtor—God bless the suburban telegraph.

That's when the real bustle began. Over the following weeks, Bill and Nancy's modest yellow colonial turned into a parking lot of pickup trucks and moving vans hauling off huge cardboard boxes, bedroom sets, and a well-loved armchair covered in kelly green corduroy, all orchestrated by a very robust, very in-charge woman who definitely was not Nancy.

Like a squirrel in a tree, I continued watching curiously from my desk in the bedroom. The large van parked next to the boss lady, who was busy organizing different piles along the driveway: old children's bicycles, picture frames, books, and golf bags, including the old leather kind that must've weighed over forty pounds, as well as an armory of tools that belonged to Bill's weathered workbench and dozens of plastic bins with what looked like decorations from Easter, Memorial Day, and every other noteworthy holiday.

As I leaned in closer, fixating on what other treasures might be unearthed from their garage, I suddenly saw Bill and Nancy emerge from the side door. Bill's tall, statuesque frame now slightly hunched over, his long, thin arm supported by Nancy, who was wearing one of her signature long paisley-printed dresses. I hadn't seen them, or spoken to them, since Nancy's original voicemail, which tugged at me. I had wanted to call her back, but days had turned into weeks and the mounting guilt made it that much harder. I didn't know what to say or how to say it. What if Bill and Nancy were sad about moving, the assisted living facility one stop away from unappetizing meal trays in some stale nursing home. Or worse, what if one of them was sick?

Witnessing them from my perch, their entire lives, their belongings, memories, tears, fears, and laughter being sorted, cataloged in their driveway then casually dispensed of by some anonymous woman, gripped at my heart, making it hard to breathe. I welled up with tears again. My heart ached for them having to say goodbye to a time and place they had called home for so many years, being set off to pasture in some unfamiliar, nondescript place with other old people.

It brought back a flood of raw, painful memories from cleaning out my stepmother's home after she'd died: the tag sale, the neighbors and bargain hunters offering condolences while coyly fishing for a deal. I thought about my own home, my own furniture, our closets and collections being strewn out on our lawn one day, estate sale ladies pilfering through them, defining value with a roll of red stickers. Bill and Nancy's driveway felt like a crystal ball, my husband and me one small generational hop away from geriatric care.

The rational side of me knew that Bill and Nancy's move was simply part of the circle of life. We grow up. We get old. Eventually a new generation takes hold. But the reality is that emotions are not always rational. Sometimes we feel exposed and raw. And witnessing Bill and Nancy standing in front of their home amid all their belongings was another jarring reminder that life was moving incredibly fast. Too fast. So fast that at times we're unable to catch our breath, and, if we're not careful, then suddenly it's us standing in that driveway, sorting through our own pile of memories.

My truth is that I'm nervous about what the next stage of life will look like. I worry about the eerie silence of empty bedrooms and fleeting phone calls from our kids, and whether my husband and I will grow old together or drive each other away. I worry about where my husband and I will go when we can't be in our house any longer or how we will manage if one of us gets sick. Don't get me wrong, I'm also incredibly excited and curious. I know that there are many exhilarating new chapters ahead—creatively, personally, and professionally—but there are moments when the unknown, tangled up with a decomposing umbilical cord as my teenagers seemingly need me less and less, makes my chest hurt and my throat tighten.

The deeper truth, or the one that I hadn't realized before, was that suddenly *I* was the oldest woman on the street now. Literally. *How did that happen?* I wondered. I didn't feel old. I subscribed to the notion that age is an attitude, not a number, and my attitude hovered around twenty-eight. I listened to podcasts and managed multiple Instagram accounts. I was an expert Zara shopper (even my daughter's friends commented on my cute outfits!). But even so, I couldn't shake the feeling that a gigantic, oversized *Alice in Wonderland*–style hourglass had flipped upside down, its sand quickly running out.

Bill and Nancy's move weighed on me for months. The notion that time was finite felt like a mushrooming cloud hovering over me when I saw babies in the park, my reflection in the mirror, my mom at the doctor, or a friend at a funeral. Weeks later when my friend Paula and I were out walking, I told her about Bill and Nancy. I started to cry again. She listened gracefully and reminded me about her own trick for unpacking complicated issues. She asked herself, *What would my therapist say?*

I liked therapy, all kinds. I loved unraveling complex emotions, the guidance, the perspective from a seasoned professional who was invested in my personal growth, the roundabout questioning they'd ask to help me probe deeper inside myself. *What would my therapist say?* I thought as I continued to hold space for myself. One thing was becoming clear: The universe had sat me at my bedroom window for a reason. To pause and reflect. To go inward. As I did that, I let my emotions continue to move through me. Bill and Nancy were in a transition, and so was I.

I was in a "middle place." Not as young as I used to be, but not old either. It felt unfamiliar and messy. I kept listening to my inner voice, imagining a therapist saying something like "Yes, you're right, your life is messy right now. And it's normal to feel overwhelmed. This middle place isn't just about one transition but a myriad of transitions all seemingly happening at the same time: your mom aging, your kids growing up, your marriage evolving, friendships in flux. That's a lot of transition at once," she'd say, continuing to reassure me that I would find my way across this messy middle, but not by holding on to the younger version of myself. "Take time to mourn her, but then *LET GO*. Rely on the wisdom that you've gained from each wrinkle, adventure, and experience that you've loved and have that collective force pull you forward into this new chapter. Be curious. Be open-minded about what's ahead, and while you're following those breadcrumbs, lean into your wisdom and start sharing it. Share it with the younger moms on your street; share it with colleagues at work, at church and with friends. Continue to listen earnestly. Share emphatically and stay connected because community and friendship will be everything as we age." That's what I think she'd say.

I continue to think about Bill and Nancy, wondering how they're doing. I hear about them from others at church, and we've been over to say hi to the new neighbors. I still feel tentative about this messy middle, but having words to describe it helps. Leaning into the transition also fuels a different kind of appreciation, for my life, the home I love, and the memories I'm making, messy or not.

Midlife Vertigo: How Travel Led Me Home to Myself

SUSAN HEINRICH

When you're lost, you search for a way home—but when home is the place you are adrift, how can you begin to orient yourself, to point your life in the right direction?

There was no event or life change that caused me to feel unmoored as I approached fifty—no health crisis, job loss, or divorce. Yet I increasingly felt what I describe as "midlife vertigo." Vertigo is the feeling that you, or your environment, are moving. I was where I had always been, married to a lovely guy who made me laugh, and the mom of two sweet and appropriately taxing teen sons. Yet the cozy familiarity of my life, once a joy, now felt unsettling. Something in me was shifting, something I didn't understand.

I had gone from happy and content with my life to emotionally erratic. Hot anger would bubble up inside me during some routine task. At other times it was sadness; my heart ached for something that I couldn't name. The one constant was irritability. My husband Sean joked that it was like having a third teenager around. I sat next to him in the car with my headphones on; whatever he was listening to, I wasn't. Did I really ever enjoy the *This American Life* podcast?

Teenagers act as they do for a reason. Biology wires them to differentiate themselves, to explore their identity separate from their families. But I was a midlife mom, the sun at the center of my family's orbit. I couldn't just upend our familial gravity.

At first, I didn't connect my unhappiness to fluctuating hormones. I wasn't experiencing any of the physical changes that can accompany midlife, like hot flashes and insomnia. But I've come to learn that the season of life leading to the end of fertility (perimenopause) can cause women to experience the most intense emotional upheaval since the teen years.

As our ovaries wind down, estrogen becomes erratic. It rises and falls like an out-of-control roller coaster while we grip the safety bar and scream to get off. For some of us, the "roller coaster" is physical symptoms. For others, like me, it's emotional. It can also be both. Since declining estrogen levels can lead to changes in our brain's chemistry, it is safe to say that my changing hormones contributed to my "midlife vertigo." But that's not the whole story. I think of it this way: Hormonal changes can pull back the curtain on your life. Faced with an unadorned view, it becomes harder to ignore thorny issues that in the past you might have ignored.

I couldn't see the problems, but I could feel them. Despite my lovely life, I felt lost and unhappy. The answers I sought might have been uncovered with therapy, journaling, or any other myriad of approaches. There's never just one way forward. But my journey back to myself was a midlife expedition that took me to three continents.

India
Where travel reminded me who I was

At the height of my vertigo, I received an email from my friend Lisa with an unexpected subject line: *Come to India!* Lisa and her husband Mike planned to attend a relative's wedding in Delhi, followed by a group trip around Rajasthan. Would I like to join them on a fifteen-day guided tour? My first thought was *yes!!* And my second thought, and the seemingly correct one: There was no way. My kids were fourteen and seventeen, my husband had a demanding job, and I was the at-home parent.

I had missed out on a trip to India once before. In my twenties, friends and I had traveled together in Nepal, after which they continued to India, but because I had less time, I went to Thailand. I spent the next two decades regretting it and wondering if the chance to visit India would come again. Now, here it was. I told myself all the reasons why I couldn't go but then shared with my husband Sean how much I wanted to say yes. He encouraged me. "Go," he said. "We'll be fine."

As my departure came closer, the thought of being that far from my family for almost three weeks filled me with angst. I almost canceled the trip when reports of horrendous air quality in Delhi seemed a reason to do so.

The goodbyes were emotional (for me) and the hugs especially tight. Then with two long flights I was transported to another world. India is jarring at first—noisy *tuk tuks* and endless honking, a shocking amount of litter and heartbreaking poverty. Meanwhile cows, which are sacred to Hindus, roam the streets, free to do and eat what they like. I saw a hungry bovine eat an entire fruit pie, along with the foil plate, and another foraging through a small-town wedding venue after the guests had departed.

But just beyond the chaos we experienced India's enchantments: garlands of orange marigolds draped across shrines, women with shy smiles and colorful saris, always busy at work. Stately hilltop forts and glittering lakeside palaces—architectural marvels that tell the story of Rajasthan, India's land of kings, incredible food and delightful people who are curious and welcoming.

I like to think it was the unique magic of India, but I suspect that any place so far from home could have been the catalyst I needed at that moment in my life. Being twelve time zones from my family, my obligations, and my identity as a wife and mom allowed me to remember how it felt to simply be me—how I had once craved adventure, that it was thrilling to meet people with lives so different from my own. Being "just Susan" in India was exhilarating. I realized that over the years, I had allowed pieces of myself to float away, like the candles set atop the Ganges river in a traditional Aarti ceremony.

It's not unusual to let go of things as our lives evolve, especially if that evolution includes parenting. But I hadn't understood the impact of it until I was reacquainted with those parts of myself in India. As I flew back through twelve time zones toward home, I wondered, *Now what?* Vacations end and we resume day-to-day life. But I sensed that some sort of midlife genie was out of the bottle.

My family had managed beautifully without me. Everyone took on new responsibilities, and my younger son picked up some skills in the kitchen—impressively, he now knew the difference between parsley and cilantro.

I settled back into home life while endeavoring to create a new normal. I wanted more of how I felt in India; the craving for independence and adventure persisted.

I realized I needed to have an honest conversation with Sean. While I was in India, he had sent me a lovely email, writing, "Squeeze all the tamarind juice you can out of this awesome once-in-a-lifetime trip." I had to tell him that India hadn't cured my wanderlust; it had ignited it.

Southeast Asia
Where travel helped me see new possibilities for myself

Smell is said to be the sense that is most closely linked to our brain's memory center. On a very hot day in Penang, Malaysia, the sticky-sweet fragrance of overripe fruit mingled with the pungent tang of chiles and ginger, transporting me back more than two decades to a backpacking trip I'd taken at twenty-five. I remembered the feelings of nervous excitement, with a three-month adventure through Asia stretching ahead of me.

I had returned to Asia for the first time since my twenties and walked past temples where curls of smoke rose from incense sticks, and giant Buddhas sat in quiet contemplation. So much was as I'd remembered.

My friend Clemencia met me to explore Penang and then Cambodia. We had shared a room on the India trip, and her recent move to Hong Kong was the perfect excuse for our next adventure. Having to tell Sean I wanted to go to Asia without him was difficult. But he sensed it was important to me, for reasons neither of us entirely understood, and was supportive.

Almost two years had passed since the trip to India. It had helped me realize I needed to put myself back at the center of my own life. The first step had been to scale back some of my obligations. That gave me time to focus on things that mattered to me, such as my writing and making my health a priority. I was also trying to step out of my comfort zone more often. As a result, life now felt more aligned with who I was, the vertigo abating. Yet I still had unanswered questions. I intuitively felt time on my own would help, so after my travels with Clemencia I went to Laos by myself.

Luang Prabang was the ancient capital of Laos until 1975 and is known for its Buddhist temples, monasteries, and beautiful setting at the confluence of the Mekong and Nam Khan rivers. I dropped my bags at the hotel and set out to explore with my camera. I took time to contemplate the light, to adjust the camera settings to pull different things in and out of focus. Such leisurely exploration in a beautiful place felt inspiring.

The next morning, I waited in darkness for a procession of Buddhist monks to appear; a hint of purple at the horizon suggested the sun would soon rise. In the distance, the shadows seemed to shift, and I saw a first glimpse of saffron. A long line of monks soon came into view. Dressed in orange robes, they walked, barefoot and silent, toward a row of townspeople who were seated or crouched and held woven pots filled with sticky rice and other offerings. I waited, too, with my own bowl of rice.

As each monk passed, I placed a small scoop of rice into the alms bowl that hung from his shoulder. This daily ritual is known as *Tak Bat* in Lao and dates back centuries. It is seen as mutually beneficial; the monks are fed, and the devotees earn karma, helping to pave their way into the next life. I'll say this about almsgiving: It's harder than it looks. The monks' pace is steady, so if you lose your rhythm for even a moment, the bowl has moved just out of reach. I marveled at their contentment with such a simple life. How must that feel?

With the almsgiving complete, I picked up my camera and went to the local market. I took photos of colorful textiles, fermented fish wrapped in green banana leaves, and crisp bugs ready for snacking on. I thought about how I had never considered myself a photographer. Why not? I pondered this question in the days to come. As in India, with distance from home, I was able to imagine new possibilities for myself. I remembered being twenty-five and believing that almost anything was possible. By the end of my trip to Asia, the midlife me had started to believe it too.

*****

On New Year's Day 2020, two months after my Asia trip, I wrote four words on my mirror: "Be Kind to Yourself." After returning home, I had applied for some jobs, with no luck. In speaking with other women my age who were trying to pivot to new careers, it became clear that ageism was real. With each rejection, my inner critic got louder. I decided that 2020 was the year I would toss aside limiting beliefs, among them the belief that it was too late to change my life.

Meanwhile, my children were growing up, my oldest now at college, so 2020 was also the year we would take a special family trip to Morocco. And then a strange new virus upended the world.

Hunkered down during the pandemic, I couldn't travel, but I could write about travel. I had talked to many women who were baffled to learn of the trips I had taken without my husband or family. *Didn't I feel selfish?* they inevitably asked. I was still making sense of my journey and also questioning why women so often put their needs behind everyone else's. Writing was a way to share my experiences—my messy midlife vertigo and the parts of myself I was rediscovering through travel.

In the summer of 2020, at the height of the pandemic, I launched Midlife Globetrotter, a website for women who wanted to add travel and adventure to their lives. Worse timing was hard to imagine. At that point, I still didn't know exactly where I was headed, but travel had reminded me how to accept uncertainty, and I knew that it made me feel more alive, inspired, and free. Maybe I was still adrift, but I was learning to trust the compass of my intuition.

Paris
Where I became my own best friend

In the fall of 2021, as people began tiptoeing back to travel, I went to Paris for ten days on my own. I had returned to French classes during the pandemic—one of my long-held dreams is to become conversational in French—and one of my favorite French words is *flâneur*. It means a person who strolls aimlessly, without agenda or destination. There's no equivalent word in English. After so much time at home, I wanted to immerse myself in a beautiful place unencumbered by any particular plan.

With my improved language skills and the luxury to explore as I wished, my affection for Paris blossomed. Every day was perfect. I lingered at the open-air market on Boulevard Raspail on a Tuesday morning for the fun of overhearing elegantly dressed patrons inquire about the provenance of the apples or the ripeness of the Camembert. Museum visits were leisurely or brief, depending on my mood. I lingered in streetside cafés, watched the Eiffel Tower glitter, and dressed up and took myself on a Seine dinner cruise. In Paris, I enjoyed my own company as I never had before.

I returned from Paris with a new feeling of contentment, with myself and my life: I had reached my own sort of midlife *belle époque*, or beautiful age. It's not that all my questions were answered, but I felt immense gratitude and acceptance for my life and the stage I was at.

Southern Africa
Where travel taught me to accept life's duality

In the spring of 2023, I went to Africa for the first time, a trip I had dreamed of my whole life. The main reason for my trip was to visit a dear friend in South Africa. Work obligations kept her from joining me on a safari, so I traveled to neighboring Botswana on my own. Botswana is blessed with stunning and diverse landscapes within a relatively small area. It also has the second-largest zebra migration on the continent, after the one in East Africa. The timing of this phenomenon varies; it depends on the seasonal rains that bring the lush grassland the zebras graze on.

When I planned my trip, I knew it was unlikely that the zebras' arrival at the vast Makgadikgadi salt pans would coincide with my own. But one day our jeep turned a corner, and there they were, hundreds of zebras wading in a shallow river. The herd was like a living work of art—individually their stripes are mostly symmetrical, but together they were a huge black and white abstract, framed by the lush green valley. A zebra herd is sometimes referred to as a "dazzle," and I understood why.

In that special moment I felt a wistful sadness. It came quickly, like the anguish I couldn't make sense of at the height of my vertigo. But this I understood. I gazed at the zebras and thought that an experience this magical should be shared with people you love. I wanted my husband and kids in that jeep with me. I enjoyed the rest of the trip, but that feeling of wishing they were there never left me.

This is the duality I now accept in my life, that two seemingly opposite things can coexist. I still crave solo adventures and the sense of freedom they provide, yet more and more I want to share travel with the people whom I love, my family and friends.

My midlife travels have been an incredible gift. They allowed me to rendezvous with the parts of myself I had set aside over the years and to explore new possibilities. And they brought me home to myself, and there's no place like home.

*****

The night sky in Africa is unlike that of the northern hemisphere. If you weren't aware of this fact, you might feel disoriented when you look up and familiar constellations appear "upside down." This might cause a disorienting sort of vertigo. But then you'd remember—you are in Africa! And the unfamiliar brings the chance for new discoveries. Far from your everyday life, you might dream a new dream as you gaze at the upside-down stars. If you're willing to venture into the unknown, something new is surely waiting for you. A dazzle of zebras might be around the next corner.

Excavating the Leader

MICHELLE JACOBS

I have had a job since I was fifteen. After getting that first pay-check, there was no going back. In high school, I worked at every store in the mall, from The Gap to Barnes & Noble to J.Crew. In college, I waitressed at the one restaurant in town where everyone went before formals and parties. I loved it.

As I got older, it progressed from there. I moved up to bigger and better things: Pfizer, *Real Simple* magazine, HSN. Big jobs. Lots of responsibility. I was good at work. Like many women, I plowed through my to-do lists and took on extra projects, believing that was the key to glowing reviews and promotions. And my bosses always liked me, a reliable team player, enthusiastic about the company (even when undeserved). Plus, I never asked for too much. A compliment on my hard work ethic and positive relationships filled me up. I look back now and shudder at my naivete and lack of awareness of how much I did and how little I received in return; regardless, that was who I was—the ultimate worker bee. Load me up and I will get the work done.

In 2020, I finally had enough. I found myself standing on the train platform near my home in Westchester, New York, completely bundled against a snowstorm that had hit "snow hurricane" levels. My (male) boss had emailed me: "Everyone else made it in," he'd written. "Not sure why you can't." So I left my kids and husband warm at home and trudged off into the city—because that was what I did. I never said no, and I did what *I thought* was expected of a truly committed staffer. But this time was different. I looked around, noticed I was alone, wet, and freezing, and knew I was done. I saw for the first time what I really was: totally burned out.

After years of launching brands and companies for other people, I realized in that moment that I could do it for myself. I knew then and there, standing on that platform, that I couldn't possibly work for another person again. Luckily, I had a smart friend, a work friend, who had also toiled in corporate America for decades, and she wanted to start a company with me. We'd each built successful millennial brands in almost every category, from home furnishings to clean skincare. We had networks that were wide and deep. And we'd both watched our bodies age and change, and recognized that there were no modern, everyday products out there for women like us. We believed we had the skills needed to start a company and develop a brand—a modern approach to aging with skincare, supplements, and sexual wellness products.

The first few months of shaping our company were perfect, even as we did it in the middle of a pandemic. My business partner said I was "like a dog with a bone"—give me a list of projects and they'd all be checked off immediately. Focus groups? Easy. Product development research? Piece of cake. Finding someone to source an ingredient? I could comb LinkedIn like no one else. This was where I shined.

We found amazing people to team up with, and I knew exactly how to get the work done. So when people asked how we were able to build Womaness during COVID times from home, I laughed. This was my forte, and I relished it. Being busy and solving the problems we encountered was my sweet spot. I reached out to people I hadn't spoken to in years. Because I had always been such a good worker and doer, people believed in me and what we were building. "If anyone can do it, it's you," I'd often hear. "Michelle, you have always found a way."

We officially launched Womaness in March of 2021. It was hard and scary, but we did it. We had thirteen products and a website full of relevant and important information for women. I was so proud of what we'd created. But the launch brought new-to-me responsibilities. I had to speak to investors. I had interviews with the press. I had a team of people to lead. I had to appear on TV. I was *a founder*. I was booked on panels with other founders and asked about my leadership, my courage. *How did I find the motivation to build Womaness? What was my vision for the future? What drove me, and what was my personal mission?*

The worker bee in me felt something new: I was stuck. To my surprise, I noticed myself deferring to my business partner. Seeing myself as someone always in the trenches, I somehow couldn't grasp that I had played a huge role in growing Womaness from the ground up—from the idea, the vision, and the mission to the tangible products. The worker didn't see herself as a founder or a leader. I was still looking for a boss, the person to tell me what a great job I had done. I felt lost and, frankly, scared.

The weeks went on, and the daily stress and pressure of running a business grew. I saw my partner juggling too many things while I retreated into my comfort zone of to-do lists. I knew it wasn't fair—to her or to me—and I knew I needed to shift how I saw myself, particularly in this new work context. I wanted Womaness to be my moment to rise up, to be a better leader than those I had experienced within the corporate world. I wanted my network of people to know I could do this. If I didn't figure this out, I would fall back into my old ways. I'd be a list-checker instead of a leader.

It was harder than I had ever anticipated. And it was so difficult to break my habits that I knew I needed help. I reached out to an executive coach, meeting with her once a week for about eight weeks. She pushed me to ask myself questions. *Why couldn't I speak for Womaness? Why did I need to defer to someone else? Why did I need to hear "good job" to believe I did well at work?*

Some of the most important things we discussed centered around "why me?" Why were other people qualified to be founders and business experts, but I wasn't—at least, according to me? There definitely was a little "fake it 'till you make it" I had to learn, but now I was the expert in Womaness. I knew this brand and all that went with it inside and out. Why wasn't I acknowledging that I was just as qualified to talk about starting a company as anyone? And what would happen if I stepped up—if I talked about my vision and helped set the course instead of quietly standing back?

Facing hard questions head on and shifting the way I thought about myself shifted *me*. But it didn't happen all at once. It wasn't a moment of pivot or an *aha*. It was gradual. Having success on TV and witnessing myself come off clearly and concisely on screen helped. Watching my team thrive under my leadership made me feel that I was finally able to be the strong leader I'd always wanted. Most importantly, my relationship with my business partner changed. She soon relied on me to share in all the responsibilities. If she couldn't make a call, she knew I could handle it (and so did I). Whoever could make an interview or press moment would grab it. I didn't slink back into the shadows but now stood next to her as an equal and offered to take on more. That was when the shift occurred. Yes, I still enjoyed a quiet day of working my way down a list of to-dos. But I also loved when my partner and I both shined while discussing our experiences and the creation of our truly groundbreaking company.

This process continues even today, four years in. I have gained more confidence as I've reflected on all we've accomplished. When I sit in a room with other business leaders, I speak with expertise and wisdom. People look to me for my experience, and I have started to embrace this role. We have been through a lot of ups and downs as founders and brand builders. I enjoy sharing our story. But what I really love is telling other women that they can do it too.

Many women, when starting out, are like me. Real worker bees. Getting stuff done and hoping for the promotion. Some do get the impressive jobs and move to bigger and better things; some remain, often at the director level, drudging away, hoping for the "good job" compliment. What I tell those women is that all their experiences have prepared them for their next big thing, that vision they can't stop daydreaming about. And when the time comes, they CAN step up into a new role. They are just as qualified as anyone to be encouraging leaders and inspiring visionaries if they want to be.

Sometimes it's about envisioning yourself differently. And talking to yourself differently. Telling yourself, *I am prepared. I am ready to do this. I am an expert in this field.* It sounds simple, but it's often not. Self-doubt sometimes creeps back in, but that leader, entrepreneur, or whomever it is you are imagining is in you. And when *you* believe it, the rest of the world will nod their heads and say, "Of course. I always knew she was a rock star."

CHAPTER 2

Empty-ish Nest

When Birds Fly the Coop

*There are two gifts we should give our children:
one is roots, and the other is wings.*
—*Unknown*

Empty Nesting

WENDI AARONS

What nobody tells you about your nest emptying is how long it takes for the nest to actually empty. Birds just shove their little fledglings out of their branch-and-stick beds whenever they think the time has come for them to fly, hoping their wings work. Humans, not so much.

I spent months "helping" my oldest son Sam apply to colleges. Most of it was in the form of nagging, which happens to be one of my best soft skills, but it was still a hassle. As anyone with a teenager knows, getting into college now isn't as simple as it used to be. I'm pretty sure that in 1986 I just mailed a postcard to University of Oregon that said, "I want in, thanks. Duran Duran rules!" Now kids have to write a resume detailing all of the nonprofit foundations they started and essays detailing the many kidneys they donated, and answer questions like "How will you change the trajectory of the entire planet and also humankind with your accounting degree?" There's no shortage of college services, counselors, and experts you can throw money at to supposedly make the process easier, but here's the thing: It's never easy.

But we somehow managed to get his applications in by the various schools' deadlines, and then, after a few nail-biting weeks, the acceptances and rejections rolled in like a traveling circus. Like most kids, he had highs and lows and a few "how didn't I get in but (insert name of hated classmate) did?" frustrations, but ultimately he had some great options. None of them were all-expenses-paid options, but good options nonetheless.

That spring, Sam graduated from high school (via Zoom, because he was part of the fun pandemic class of 2020) and then finally made his decision on where he wanted to spend the next four years. We were all happy to hear that it wasn't going to be his bedroom because by then, after a lot of family quarantining, I was ready to turn it into a meditation room with a wet bar and maybe a sensory deprivation tank or two.

Part one of the empty-nesting process done, we moved on to part two: the Readying of the Empty Nest, AKA Preparing for Liftoff.

Many pregnant women, myself included, go through a period called "nesting" as the baby's arrival nears. This is when you buy all of your necessities and fix up the nursery so that it looks adorable. Empty nesting is similar, only now you buy necessities for the baby to use in his dorm room that will never be described as adorable. Well, maybe if you have a daughter who loves pink and goes to a southern college, but not so much in our case. We got busy buying from Amazon, Bed Bath and Beyond, and Target, and soon everything he needed was ready to be shipped to his school. But as the date grew nearer for *him* to be shipped to school, I realized that he was ready to leave, but me, not so much.

I thought I was prepared, but as the drop-off date approached, I also began to feel separation anxiety creep in. I'd lie in bed, wide awake at 3 a.m. with my mind and pulse racing. Would he miss me? Would he remember to call home? Would I just sit in his empty room, humming "Sunrise, Sunset" and wondering what to do with my life now that I wasn't a full-time mom for the first time in eighteen years? A lower grocery bill is great, but it definitely doesn't make up for not having your kid living at home anymore. *Is this why people have eighteen kids?* I'd think. *So there's always one at home?*

I pushed those thoughts out of my head while we made the final preparations, and drop-off day finally arrived. With my heart in my throat, we moved Sam into his bright dorm room that would soon not smell so nice. Then came the time to say goodbye. I'd kept it together all day, without even a single tear escaping, but I suddenly found myself fighting the urge to cling to his knees. He'd clung to mine the first day of kindergarten until I was honest with my emotions and reminded him (and myself) that it was tough, but he'd love school. Now, fourteen years later, the roles were reversed, and I was the one who felt like I was being abandoned.

I took a deep breath and managed to squeak out, "I'm so proud of you, sweetie. I'm also kind of sad." He gave me a sweet smile and reassured me, and maybe himself, "We're both going to do great, Mom." And almost four years later, I have to say that we have. Even though I never managed to build that wet bar in his bedroom.

I like to think of the first days of kindergarten and college drop-off as Boo-Hoo/Yahoos. Because while they may be a sad end to one chapter of the parent–child relationship, they're also the start of amazing new adventures for you both.

It's Getting Too Quiet

It's mid-September, and I've just dried my eyes after dropping off my seventeen-year-old twins at their boarding schools. It doesn't get easier. I know their schools are the perfect places for them—but that doesn't mean emotionally I'm always happy about it.

My younger son, age nine, and I walked upstairs yesterday morning as he rubbed his sleepy eyes. It was the first morning the twins were gone. "Oh, look," he said, glancing at their empty rooms. "So sad! The rooms are both empty!" I couldn't have said it better myself.

As a divorced mom, I got an early indoctrination to the quiet that descends when the kids leave. Every other weekend, I wrestled with the stillness. Ironically, the calm I longed for when all four of them were home was unwelcome when I knew I couldn't be with them. I was either overwhelmed or devastated. Some weekends I still bawl my eyes out.

But this September, school sadness lodges itself into my chest. The kids are happy. They've sent photos. They beam on FaceTime. And so, I am "happy." I just miss them. I miss having them at the dinner table. I miss the meals we all could've had together but, instead, it'll just be the two younger kids. Which is great! They're adorable and funny and a handful. It just isn't the same.

I miss the moments that we don't share. The early mornings. The late nights. Sitting on the couch next to my son while he plays video games. Helping my daughter pick an outfit...or a phone case...or a water bottle. I miss all of us crammed in an elevator together trying not to step on the dog. I miss the jokes, the jabs, the jests.

Mostly, I miss the hugs. My kids say I give the best hugs, but it's really them. My arms feel so empty when I can't regularly hug the kids that I sometimes sleep with Hot Cocoa, my stuffed animal monkey.

And their rooms: What do I do with them? They're so.... neat. I barely recognize them without clothes on the floor. Sometimes I go in and sit on their beds. I hug their pillows. I smell their sweatshirts.

This sounds pathetic. My kids are, thank God, alive and well.

When my son first went to boarding school, my husband and I were at Shabbat services with the other kids. When the rabbi asked those who were in mourning to please rise, I sobbed.

"He's still with us," my husband said. "It's OK." Yes, our kids are still with us, but they're not here. It's different.

I am mourning. I mourn the loss of the everyday. The casual encounters. The daily dramas. I mourn the passing of time even as I celebrate it. I mourn the loss of my identity as a mom as the kids catapult into college-land. *Who will I be without them?*

Early this morning, a day when I don't have the kids, I walked the dog on the street at the exact moment kids from all different schools were waiting with their parents for the bus. It was just Nya and me. I smiled and waved, said hi to those I knew, and lingered awkwardly before going upstairs. I longed to be part of it, still. I even waited in my lobby until the bus in front of the house pulled away. And then I sighed and took the elevator upstairs, alone. The laughs not heard. The moments not shared.

It was my turn. And now my turn is ending. I can see it, the light at the end of the tunnel that as a new mom struggling to get through the day, I couldn't believe would ever come. But now that it's here? I feel both utterly and completely proud of my kids and who they've become, while also hollow, knowing that one of the most meaningful times of my life is coming to a close.

Of course, I'll always be a mom—and hopefully, one day, a grandmother to many. I'll always light up when I see one of the kids calling or FaceTiming. I'll still be dealing with so much of their lives. But they'll be on their own.

My son got his driver's license this summer. He is ready. Am I?

CHAPTER 3

Hotter Than Ever

Peri/Menopause Tales and Advice

*There is no more creative force in the world
than the menopausal woman with zest.*
—*Margaret Mead*

Toxic Rage

KATIE FOGARTY

"I want a divorce."

Four words detonating a sunny day, shouted in my gravel driveway at my college boyfriend husband of twenty-four years. He looked shocked.

I felt crazy. How had I gotten to this moment, this mad utterance?

Together, we had traveled miles of good road since the night I perched on the sticky kitchen counter of his off-campus college apartment, legs locked around his waist, and declared, "I am in love with you." He looked shocked then too.

No midlife marriage heads into a third decade undented and unscratched, but for years we moved in (mostly) happy synchronicity, buoyed through life's ups and downs by a shared wiring toward optimism and the fact that we liked one another. Mix in a soft cushion of dot-com stock options and a semiofficial operating agreement that only one person was allowed to be crazy at a time, and we had a recipe that worked.

But suddenly, I felt crazy, most of the time.

I didn't want a divorce—I wanted a good night's sleep. And lots of them, strung together like a beaded necklace garlanding me with sanity, impulse control, and fewer racoon under-eye circles. I wanted to sleep like my husband, who hit the pillow and was snoring within seconds.

I craved an end to the pandemic: to the fear that choked me awake at 4 a.m., the relentless familial togetherness, the dystopian apartness from everyone else. I was exhausted on a cellular level—tired of Cloroxing the groceries, the WTF news cycle, an amoral president, the precarious finances of a household of a consultant and a start-up founder struggling with capital raising.

I was also sick and tired of sprouting hot tears at weird times and a spin cycle of outsized emotions, sick and tired of thinking—*I need to get my shit together.*

Much later, I would learn that the slow, subterranean gears of perimenopause were grinding away my serotonin and my dopamine, warping my coping skills, reshaping my sense of self. I would also learn I was far from alone.

As the pandemic ebbed, I found myself a newly minted midlife podcaster, host of *A Certain Age*, invited to midlife conferences and menopause company launch parties, listening to women share the same steady drumbeat—*I thought I was crazy. I almost got divorced. Painful sex, loss of intimacy. Dry vagina, dry vagina, dry vagina.*

I love a good cult, a sisterhood, a team. It was comforting to feel seen, but also infuriating. I navigated three pregnancies with *What to Expect When You're Expecting* clutched in hand. Where the hell was *What to Expect When Your Estrogen Is Exiting*? I was blindsided by the magnitude of change.

Yes, I knew menopause was coming. Saturday-night teen babysitting gigs spent thumbing through other people's *Cosmopolitans* taught me about sex and vibrators, offering a women's health and sex ed barely hinted at by my Catholic high school. I knew from an early age that menopause would one day roll around with what sounded like pesky companions, hot flashes, and night sweats. Hot flashes have a very good PR agent—they are practically synonymous with menopause.

When my period disappeared at age forty-nine without a hot flash in sight, no sweaty, tangled bedsheets, I thought I was skating through.

Wrong.

Menopause's other less showy, but equally maddening symptoms—interrupted sleep, fatigue, extreme mood swings, and more—were taking a star turn. I simply didn't fully grasp that it was menopause that was wreaking havoc on my sleep, my mood, and, at times, what felt like my sanity. "We call that mood instability," said my first podcast interview, my friend Anita, an ob-gyn who delivered JLo's twins.

Mood instability sounds so genteel, like a tall glass of lemonade wobbling on the arm of a front porch rocking chair. My mood "instability" felt more like volcanic bouts of toxic fury—a California-grade forest fire laying cinematic waste to whatever's in its path.

Maybe this is my hot flash? Where the hell is the flame retardant?

Much has been written about women's anger and rage—journalist Rebecca Traister captures the transformative power of female anger as a force for collective social good in *Good and Mad: The Revolutionary Power of Women's Anger*. In *Rage Becomes Her*, Soraya Chemaly argues that not only is women's anger justified, but anger is an active solution for shaking off personal and cultural shackles. We can thank women's anger for suffragette voting rights, the Montgomery bus boycott, and the rise of the gun control movement.

To be clear: My bouts of lava-hot fury did not feel like a force for good. It was scary to be the owner of an emotional regulation system that kept fritzing out, cycling somewhere between low warning sparks and full-on systems failure.

At one point during an early pandemic baking spree, as my husband and I had a top-decibel fight over baking soda, my teens shrank away to their bedrooms, and I retreated to my bed at 7 p.m. with a glass of wine, sharing the fight's increasingly lunatic timeline with a text thread of high school girlfriends.

"I just want the pandemic to be over," I cried through pixels. "And the baking soda to be kept in the right place, obvs."

Our single friend Melissa typed back, "This is the first time since the pandemic started that I'm happy I'm sheltering in place alone."

I need to get my shit together.

Slowly, my husband and I made some changes. We had honest, uncomfortable conversations and, as the world reopened, carved out time for short trips away as a couple. We took low-pressure dates walking our unruly pandemic puppy. He tabled the start-up and got a new job. We learned the life-changing magic of a great lube. I worked on less wine, better sleep—trading the panic-inducing evening news for bedtime reading with blue-light blocking glasses and a dropperful of CBD oil. Time passed, and I became more steady, solid.

One of my podcast guests, the social justice and menopause advocate Omisade Burney-Scott, calls menopause a "liminal experience": a state of seismic transition—ambiguous, disorientating—that is both physical and emotional. But like any other portal (even a pandemic), the liminal space is ultimately traversed, and emergence occurs.

When I look back to that moment in the driveway just three or four years ago, it exists in both sepia-tinge and Kodachrome;

a vivid snapshot of a slice of time that feels so utterly past, an artifact of history.

My husband and I are planting flowering containers and planning for an empty nest—*Where shall we move? Maine, Portugal?* And I am doubled over in silent shaking laughter as he helps me shoot an Instagram reel for my podcast in the produce aisle of a supermarket. How did I get here, holding an artichoke, convulsed with laughter at this madly delicious moment with the man I love?

A Letter to My Premenopausal Self

DR. MARY CLAIRE HAVER

Reflecting on my journey through menopause, I can't help but acknowledge how I took this phase of life for granted. I held onto the misguided belief that I would effortlessly fall into the category of women who sail through it with ease. I equated thinness with good health, thus assuming I'd dodge the challenging aspects. But reality had other plans. The unmistakable symptoms began to unfold: the hot flushes would wash over me at the most inconvenient times, drenching sweats that were impossible to manage discreetly, sleep disruptions that left me perpetually fatigued, and the unexpected musculoskeletal pains that turned the ordinary into aches. Strangely, even in the face of mounting evidence, I found myself gaslighting my own experiences, unwilling to accept that these could be markers of menopause. It's intriguing how our minds can deny what our bodies are clearly telling us.

Through my journey, I've come to appreciate how personal and unique the experience of menopause truly is. Just as I once did, my patients often approach this phase with preconceived notions about how it will unfold based on societal narratives or generalizations. Menopause is so much more than just bothersome hot flashes and the cliché "whiney woman" trope. It represents an abrupt change in our metabolic health as well—our lipid metabolism, insulin resistance, and body composition all struggle.

However, I now understand that menopause is far from a one-size-fits-all experience. Each woman's journey is a tapestry woven from her individual symptoms and vulnerabilities. For me, the specters of osteoporosis and heart disease loom large, casting a shadow on my health concerns. But as I've discovered, a fellow traveler's path might be guided by other issues, like the risk of dementia or diabetes. Recognizing this diversity has taught me the importance of approaching menopause with empathy and a keen awareness of each person's unique needs. After all, this phase is not just a universal phenomenon; it's an intricate interplay of biology, emotions, and individuality.

So, Mary Claire, what would I tell you at thirty-five? Enjoy these years, your babies, your family, your friends, your job, your marriage. Because at some point, sooner than you can imagine, your babies will grow and leave you, two of your brothers and your father will die, your friends will divorce, your job will change (twice), and your marriage will get worse, then better. As you struggle to balance everything in your life, don't forget yourself—your mental, emotional, and physical health. Menopause is coming, and it is going to challenge your resilience in ways you never imagined—so to prepare for this, do the following:

Shift from Thin to Strong

There was a time when I fixated on the elusive goal of being thin, mistakenly equating it with beauty and self-worth. Shifting my mindset from the pursuit of thinness to embracing strength has been a transformative journey, one that has reshaped not only my physical health but also my self-esteem and overall well-being. My previous thinking took a toll on my mental health that was palpable as I became ensnared in a cycle of unrealistic expectations and self-criticism. It wasn't until I embarked on a new path, one focused on cultivating strength, that I began to truly thrive. Rather than measuring success by numbers on a scale, I started to gauge my progress through my ability to conquer physical challenges, whether it was lifting heavier weights, completing a challenging hike, or simply feeling invigorated after a workout.

This shift wasn't just about aesthetics; it was a radical transformation of my mindset. Exercising for strength and endurance became a celebration of what my body could achieve, fostering a sense of empowerment that far surpassed the fleeting satisfaction of fitting into a smaller dress size. I began to focus on activities that would lead to my function and independence in my seventies and eighties—and realized that trying to stay "small" would chip away at my bone and muscle strength.

Moreover, as I delved into strength training, I uncovered the remarkable benefits it offered for bone health. Recognizing that strong muscles support strong bones, I understood that this practice wasn't just about the present but an investment in my future as well. With each weight lifted and each milestone achieved, I was crafting a foundation for a functional and vibrant life as I aged. This shift from thin to strong has taught me that vitality isn't confined to a particular body shape; it radiates from a body that's nurtured, challenged, and respected for its capabilities.

Nutrition Over Calories

The relentless pursuit of calorie reduction once monopolized my thoughts, inadvertently taking a toll on my mental well-being. Transitioning my perspective from fixating on calorie counts to embracing the nutritional value of food has marked a profound evolution in my approach to health. This principle stands as a cornerstone in my book *The Galveston Diet*, a testament to my realization that true health encompasses more than mere numbers. I've discovered the significance of directing our focus toward nutrient-rich foods as the ultimate nourishment for our bodies. It's about understanding that each bite holds the potential to fuel our vitality and invigorate our existence.

In advocating this shift, I encourage others to embark on a journey where nutrients take precedence over numbers. Menopause, a chapter fraught with its unique challenges, has illuminated the importance of this approach. Certain nutrients possess an uncanny ability to become allies in managing symptoms and bolstering overall well-being. By introducing a variety of colorful fruits and vegetables into my diet, I've harnessed the power of antioxidants to combat oxidative stress, a common culprit during this transition. Embracing healthy fats has offered respite from the hormonal fluctuations that often accompany menopause. Omega-3 fatty acids, for instance, have emerged as potent supporters of heart health and cognitive function. This journey has reinforced the notion that our bodies are a canvas upon which we can paint a vibrant mosaic of wellness through mindful, nutrient-conscious choices.

Educate Yourself About Menopause

Reflecting on my own medical training, and that of countless other OB-GYN residents, it becomes painfully evident how little emphasis was placed on the comprehensive care of menopausal patients beyond their surgical requirements. I urge everyone, as I do my fellow physicians, to take a proactive stance in educating themselves about menopause. This knowledge gap isn't limited to medical professionals; it pervades society at large, underscoring the dire need for a collective awakening. The impact of this ignorance is profound, as it leaves countless women grappling with physical and emotional challenges without the support and understanding they deserve. Even in my position, I was not immune to the needless suffering. It's imperative to shed light on this crucial phase of a woman's life, unraveling its complexities and dispelling the myths that shroud it. By actively seeking accurate information, we have the power to reshape the narrative surrounding menopause. Debunking the misconceptions that perpetuate is a vital step toward ensuring women receive the care and empathy they need. To navigate this transformative journey, I encourage the utilization of reputable resources that offer insights into both the physical and emotional changes accompanying menopause. One such invaluable source is menopause.org, a platform that provides a wealth of knowledge and guidance for women, medical professionals, and families alike. In striving for a society that champions holistic understanding, we pave the way for women to embrace menopause with confidence and resilience, fostering a new era of well-informed care and support.

Consider Aging as a Privilege

I found myself embracing this notion firsthand as I embarked on a complete career transformation in my fifties, shifting from traditional private practice to a newfound focus on menopause care. I realized the importance of challenging the prevailing societal narrative that unjustly paints aging with a brush of negativity and decline. Instead, let's recognize the profound privilege that comes with the passage of time.

This transition showcased the unique opportunities that unfold with age, proving that our journey doesn't plateau; it flourishes in new and unexpected directions. Age doesn't merely tally years; it accumulates wisdom, self-assuredness, and a wealth of life experiences that mold us into the individuals we're meant to be. With each passing day, we amass a treasury of stories, insights, and perspectives that form the cornerstone of a life well-lived. It's time to dismantle the stereotype of aging as a downhill slide and instead recognize it as an exhilarating ascent to a peak of authenticity, fulfillment, and boundless potential.

Focus on Function and Longevity

Once I redirected my attention away from the relentless obsession with weight, I was able to focus on cultivating functional fitness and embracing the prospect of a long, vibrant life. While societal pressures often push us toward the pursuit of a particular body size, it's crucial to recognize that a healthy body transcends numbers on a scale. Preserving muscle mass, nurturing flexibility, and nurturing cardiovascular health emerge as the keystones of a fulfilling life journey. By investing in these facets of well-being, we pave the way for improved mobility, agility, and overall vitality as the years progress.

Maintaining muscle mass isn't just about aesthetics; it's a safeguard against frailty and an investment in autonomy. Engaging in strength-building exercises, such as resistance training, not only fortifies our physical foundation but also bolsters our mental resilience. Incorporating regular stretching routines enhances flexibility, allowing us to move through life with grace and ease. Cardiovascular health, nurtured through activities like brisk walking, swimming, or dancing, not only contributes to a strong heart but also fuels a strong sense of well-being.

Incorporating these principles into daily life need not be overwhelming. Simple habits like taking the stairs instead of the elevator, practicing yoga for enhanced flexibility, and engaging in outdoor activities that elevate the heart rate can effortlessly blend into our routines. Shifting our focus from the numbers on the scale to functional fitness not only benefits our physical health but also frees us from the constraints of societal norms. Let's redefine success in terms of strength, vitality, and the ability to embrace each day with enthusiasm, reminding ourselves that the journey toward longevity is a journey toward embracing our most authentic and capable selves.

So, Mary Claire, I say this with love: You won't see menopause coming, and it will rock your world. It will challenge your mental health, your beliefs, and your relationships. Through your own battles with menopause, you will fight to peel away the shroud of mystery that surrounds it, emphasizing the significance of education in shaping our experiences.

Empowerment lies within your grasp. Remember, every stage of life is a journey worth embracing, and the choices we make today can pave the way for a vibrant and fulfilling future.

It's All in Your Head

MARIAN ADAMS

Fingers locked tightly, my husband holds my bony hand as we ride the hospital elevator. Knots tighten in my stomach with each passing floor. Stark fluorescent lights and chalk-white walls greet us on the eleventh floor, along with a stone-faced security guard who enters a passcode, opening a huge steel door. Two white coats and a nurse look up from the long table. The nurse approaches me. "Raise your arms," she says. With shiny sharp scissors in hand, she cuts the drawstring of my yoga pants, then the laces from my running shoes.

Welcome to my nightmare. I am in the psych ward.

It's 2016, and I'm fifty-two years old. Since the age of forty, I had been the poster child for healthy living. Each morning began with a long run, weightlifting, or Vinyasa yoga. Invigorated and clear-headed, I dove into the tasks and challenges of the day. Each evening, I prepared the night's Mediterranean dish for my beloved husband and three children. It truly was "a Wonderful Life."

One of the highlights during these years was our family tradition of attending the annual Army/Navy football game. The anticipation was as much fun as the game, packing fleece blankets and roast beef on rye, pulling out the Navy hats, sweatshirts, and thermals. This Navy-loving clan would be there, rain, snow, or sunshine.

But in 2015, I felt as if someone else was watching the game. While I had always marveled at the Blue Angels soaring through the clouds and became giddy as Navy Seals parachuted onto the field, this time, there seemed to be a veil between me and the action. I could not feel the excitement, did not belt out the National Anthem as I did every year before. When my husband bounced back and forth between our seats and those a few rows away where our children sat, I felt paranoid, believing he didn't want to sit beside me. Caught up in the thrill of the game, no one noticed how frightened I was.

What was happening to me?

A few days later, while paying for my chocolate almond protein shake, the owner of our local health food store noticed my low energy, the sadness in my eyes, and said, "You're not yourself today." I wasn't.

When my sister-in-law dropped by the house the following month, she seemed concerned by my gaunt appearance and the absence of my smile. I overheard her tell my husband, "My God, she's a shell of herself." I was.

Then, one Friday afternoon at the hair salon, I suddenly began to weep uncontrollably. Fleeing to the ladies' room, I called a friend, begging for a lifeline. She didn't know what to do.

I had tried so hard to be strong and pretend everything was fine but could no longer keep up the façade—for myself or those around me. There was something seriously wrong.

Probably the most debilitating aspect of my freefall was my inability to sleep. When my husband's alarm went off at 5 a.m., as it had every weekday of our married life, I found myself, tortuously, still wide awake since the night before.

Desperate, I began attending the weekday 8 a.m. mass at St. Joseph's Roman Catholic Church, where I had been baptized fifty-two years before. On my knees, I'd light a candle for myself and beg the dear Lord, "Please help me."

And then my hair, which I've always loved, began to fall out. It was time to see a doctor. I had no idea it would be the first of many.

A friend recommended a psychiatrist, who, after a lengthy discussion and questionnaire, told me my serotonin must be very low and that I had a "mood disorder." Depression. She pumped me full of prescriptions.

After trying ten different sleep and mood medications with no relief, I went to my long-time internist, doctor No. 2. Down twenty-one pounds from my last check up, missing patches of hair on my head, I wept as I told him I couldn't sleep; I couldn't function. "A lot of people *think* they don't sleep, but they *really do*," he responded. "Besides, you can't be that bad. You're dressed nicely and wearing your pearls." He never examined me. No scale, no blood pressure, no urine sample, no stethoscope, no blood test, no EKG. Nothing. But he did hand my husband a card for the *best* psychiatrist in New York City, the doctor I went to next, who recommended electroconvulsive therapy (ECT), assuring me that 75 percent of patients with severe depression "get their lives back."

"I think you'll really like the unit," doctor No. 3 added.

And so there I was, an inpatient in the psych unit of a top Manhattan hospital. Every other day, I was instructed to undress, step into a sumo wrestler–size plastic diaper, and wrap myself in a hospital gown. Then, seated in a wheelchair, I was lined up with the other five patients waiting for the same treatment.

The room was always freezing. Just before they put me under anesthesia for the first time, I turned to one of the masked doctors. "Can you please pull the blanket over my foot?" He responded matter-of-factly, "It needs to be exposed so that we can see when it starts shaking; that signals that the seizure we are inducing in your brain has been triggered."

After more than two weeks of "treatment," I returned home. Nothing had changed.

Next stop, my gynecologist, doctor No. 4. He took one look at me and said, "I'm worried about you," and suggested I see his partner, doctor No. 5, to check my hormone balances. When I requested that she do so, she rolled her eyes and spoke to me through her assistant, in the third person. "Tell her to order Cortisol Manager, magnesium glycinate, and Methyl-Guard Plus," pricey supplements from her new website. She would not test my hormones.

I was beginning to feel hopeless but continued my search for an answer. Doctor No. 6 referred me to a neurologist, doctor No. 7, who ordered a brain MRI and a spinal tap and sent me home with an apparatus of metal discs I had to keep wrapped on my head for seventy-two hours. Verdict? No neurological issues.

Doctor No. 8 was an Ayurvedic doctor, whose examination consisted of asking me questions and looking at my tongue.

Doctor No. 9, a local female "concierge" internist, was full of condescending speculation. "Maybe it's not depression; maybe you're sad because you don't have any small children to care for anymore. You know, no reason to get up in the morning. Perhaps you should get a job." I couldn't get myself into the shower in the morning, and this woman wanted me to "get a job!"

Next, a Harvard-educated psychiatrist prescribed thirty-six rounds of transcranial magnetic stimulation. Five days a week for seven weeks, I sat in a chair with a helmet apparatus sending constant loud clicking pulses to my brain. He also suggested I take up swimming. Swimming! If I got into a pool in my state, I'd likely drown.

On what felt like my thousandth trip to Walgreens, this time to pick up gabapentin—the same medication my vet once prescribed for my ailing dog—I stared down what appeared to be an impossibly long aisle. I felt like a dead woman walking as I made my way to the pharmacy at the back of the store. I'll never forget the two female pharmacists, who'd known me when I was "myself." They spotted me and glanced at each other, and then back at me with disbelief and pity, as if they were saying, "My God, I can't believe she's here again."

By this point, I had been prescribed and taken over twenty-two different medications, including Saphris, Lexapro, Seroquel, sertraline, lamotrigine, escitalopram, clonazepam, aripiprazole, Latuda, gabapentin, Pristiq, nortriptyline, lithium carbonate, bupropion, mirtazapine, zolpidem, tranylcypromine, midodrine, and minivelle.

None of them worked. On the contrary, many, especially in combination, exacerbated my symptoms.

I had lost focus, the ability to concentrate. My mobility was impacted. My family took my car keys away.

At the lowest of lows, I began lying to my husband. "Did you walk today?" he'd ask, hoping to see even the tiniest bit of light. "Yep, mm-hmm. I walked while you were out biking," I'd say. I didn't want to disappoint him.

Almost three years since that Army/Navy game, I sat propped up on the sectional at a family gathering. My beautiful mother positioned me at the buffet, where, tongs in hand, I robotically served melon and prosciutto. I overheard a relative raving about a nutritionist he started seeing and asked for her number. Maybe she could tell me what to eat to feel a little better. The last thing I thought I needed was another doctor. But I was wrong. I needed the *right* doctor. The "nutritionist" I saw was actually an internist/endocrinologist. Dr. Carolina Sierra was doctor No. 11. And she saved my life.

In the small lab area of her office, she personally drew my blood and asked questions no other doctor had. Her clear, sapphire eyes radiated warmth, a comforting calm, and a keen intelligence. Gently placing a Band-Aid on the vein of my right arm, she turned to the nurse and said, "I want the following tests: thyroid, estrogen, progesterone, testosterone, vitamin D, vitamin B and Epstein-Barr."

Two days later, Dr. Sierra shared the results of my blood work. "Marian," she said, "the reason none of your past treatments or medications helped you is because they target a chemical imbalance in the brain, and that is not what caused your symptoms."

"You haven't slept in three years because you have no progesterone. You can't stop crying and don't feel like yourself because you have no estrogen, and no testosterone, which women need too. Your thyroid is a disaster. You have no vitamin D or vitamin B, and you did have the Epstein-Barr virus at one point." Then, with the most sincere compassion, she said, "All together, you fell off a cliff."

After nearly three years of misery, existing haggardly on the sidelines of my life, I was finally properly diagnosed. At fifty-two, along with a malfunctioning thyroid and several vitamin deficiencies, I was also in menopause, a word that not one of ten doctors over a three-year period had ever mentioned. Appropriate, targeted medications and supplements swiftly brought both my mind and body into balance and highly functioning again. Thyroid medication brought me back to a healthy weight, gave me blessed energy, and restored my lustrous locks. Compounded bioidentical hormone cream balanced my estrogen so that I could regain the joy I used to naturally feel. Replacing lost progesterone granted me dreamy, restorative sleep, and testosterone levels normalized. Prescription-strength vitamin D and daily vitamin B12 further restored my energy and mental clarity.

I felt as if I rose from the dead.

My vibrancy, humor, and health now regained, I sometimes wonder about the precious time lost with my children, husband, and exquisite, dear mother. But I don't stay there long. Rather, I turn my attention to using my experience to help other women avoid unnecessary, preventable suffering. How much could I have avoided had any of my first ten doctors been properly trained and took seriously the changes and debilitating symptoms that many women suffer when they experience menopause? By sharing my nightmare, I am turning anger into action. Above all, I tell my story to empower women. Equipped with the right questions to ask, women will be prepared to effectively advocate for their health.

"It's all in your head?" Maybe not.

Om Menopause

RACHEL HUGHES

I never would have guessed that menopause, of all things, would be the subject to bring me into true alignment with myself. My understanding of this life shift was limited solely to the fact that once in, I would no longer be capable of getting pregnant. That my years of fertility would be, in effect, over. Oh, and that death was on the horizon. Ha! What a bleak outlook, but I think one that is all too common: "Oh, no more babies? Time to dry out, shrivel up, and hunch over 'till you meet your maker!"

My interest in perimenopause and menopause began when I started experiencing symptoms about ten years ago. I was becoming unreasonably anxious when I happened upon an article in *New York* magazine titled "Midlife Psychosis" that left me feeling sentenced to losing it at some point and tethered to a hormonal ticking time bomb that had begun its countdown. Was I doomed to a future of psychiatric breaks due to hormonal fluctuations—on TOP of the hot flashes and a dry vagina? What kind of future was *that* to look forward to? I wasn't having it. And I also wasn't having the fact that too many midlife, peri/menopausal conversations I was listening to were highlighting women who looked nothing like me. Who was speaking to, and on behalf of, Black, Native, and brown women?

Black and Native women, due to systemic racism in health-care, are often misdiagnosed or receive inadequate healthcare treatment; not surprisingly, this extends to menopause. We know that Black women have a longer menopausal transition and experience more symptoms at a greater intensity than other women, and this matters to me; in fact, learning this ignited my passion and drive to do something. Because for these women, their future health and quality of life are tied directly to this fact. They have had to contend with less in the menopause context; less representation in both the research and in the overall conversation, and less access and support. This is not a reasonable reality, and becoming aware of these facts set me on my new path.

I decided to share my menopausal story, on social media no less (WHAT?!). It felt scary to expose myself so personally, but I did it anyway; once I started, everything around me began to expand. I expanded. I grew into myself, took chances I had never taken, explored my curiosities, and said *yes* more often. I thought things like "This sounds like fun.... I think I'll give this a try.... This feels like a good fit for me...." In doing so, I became comfortable in my own skin. I grew bolder and stopped hesitating to exercise my wisdom in all kinds of circumstances and relationships. I allowed myself to explore my creativity and constantly considered those things that would bring me joy. As a result, I have become healthier and happier. Honestly, I've always been healthy and happy and wise and curious and smart and capable. I just kept myself small, as so many of us do. That's all over now. And it was talking about menopause that paved my road.

The thing about peri/menopause is that it's a great time to process. It's a great time to look within and take steps that shore up your future health in all regards—your heart, brain, vaginal, and bone health, sure. But also, and this is equally important, it's time to shore up your emotional, spiritual, and mental health. Take stock and make sure you're considering the things that you eat (more plants) and the exercises you enjoy (more weights). Seek out a menopause-versed practitioner (many docs don't have menopause training, so don't assume your gyno does) to learn about menopause hormone therapy (MHT), which can be life-altering. Also consider your friendships, your boundaries, and your sleep and rest time. Think about what you're doing that brings you joy and hold to boundaries that support your mental/emotional health. Consider therapy, spend time alone, spend time with those you really enjoy, take yourself out for a meal, take seriously your desire to revisit something you long ago put down. Do more of what you want and so much less of what you don't.

The menopause transition can be challenging, but it's not insurmountable. There is a lot of fear and misunderstanding that surrounds the conversation, but I'm hoping that in some way I'm helping to correct the many outdated narratives. Whether you've experienced surgical menopause or primary ovarian insufficiency or simply want to future-proof your health as you head into midlife, this season of transition is a time to become educated and, in turn, empowered. What I'm really hoping is that in sharing all of this, I'm helping to arm not only my contemporaries but also future generations of women, and men, to step into this very normal life experience well-versed, well-informed, and unafraid.

Women and those who love them and spend time with them, at home and in workspaces, need information, education, and, ultimately, access to conversations and treatments that can help them to feel better so that they might get on with their lives.

Change is happening at a grassroots level, and the landscape is transforming; menopause is no longer a taboo topic. Conversations are finally reaching beyond the privacy of our homes and doctor's offices and onto legislative floors as women around the world have reached their threshold and demanded answers, care, support, and a normalization of the subject altogether.

As for me, I feel as though I've had a little part in this paradigm shift, and that brings me enormous joy and a real sense of purpose and responsibility. I love it. Because it happened as a result of my own midlife growth, my own interest and desire to feel better and to live a more authentic life. How amazing is that?

Everything now, in midlife, in menopause, feels limitless. It was all so unimagined and unexpected, and I would've thought feeling this way was reserved for my younger years, but I see now that I'm just getting started. YOU are just getting started. It's never too late, and your time is now.

CHAPTER 4

To Hell with the Timeline

On Late Blooming

It's never too late to be what you might have been.
—George Eliot

Naturally...A Girl

SARI BOTTON

I've never met a phase of life at which I felt right on target milestone-wise, and midlife has been no exception. I've always done everything too early or too late—mostly too late. And no matter where I've found myself along the timeline of my life, deep down I've felt like *a girl* and wanted to stay that way, even now at fifty-nine.

At certain points, like in my first, ill-advised marriage from twenty-three to twenty-six, I tried to play grownup. But I look back at those moments and see the least authentic versions of myself; I see someone trying too hard, trying to fit a certain age-appropriate mold, unsuccessfully, foolishly. I've emerged from every one of those phases like those eager to "regress" back to some semblance of girlhood—to the real me.

*****

I've felt out of step with my peers from the time I was a tween. The other girls were getting their periods then, while mine just kept not showing up. Don't get me wrong; I didn't *want* it to come. *Ever*. I hated my period long before I finally got it at eighteen.

I first learned about menstruation in 1976 in my elementary school's all-purpose room, during a sixth-grade assembly for girls only. They showed us *Naturally...a Girl*, a short film produced by Johnson & Johnson about something "very special" that happens to girls "between the ages of nine and sixteen." It was followed by a talk and Q&A, after which we were each handed paper tote bags filled with pamphlets, maxi pads, and Midol.

I didn't buy the movie's upbeat tenor. It felt forced and artificial. To me, it heralded something dark and foreboding. It said, *Get ready girls—your sweet innocent time is about to end!*

Ugh. I did *not* want to become a woman. Not yet, anyway. It wasn't my gender that was the problem. No question, I am and always have been female through and through. It was that I wanted some more time to be a child—a *girl*.

I'd already felt that precious time running out; for the past year and change, I'd been thrust into a prematurely adult role by my parents as they divorced. Misguided by that '70s tendency to treat your children like friends, they each inappropriately confided in me about their issues with the other and their difficult feelings about their marriage and divorce. They gave me latchkey-kid responsibilities I wasn't ready for, like babysitting for my little sister after school and sometimes at night, at a time when I was still afraid to be home without an adult. I was making dinner while my parents were out dating—noodles and cottage cheese, Weaver's chicken in the toaster oven, tuna salad on crackers, frozen pizza—and juggling my homework with laundry and other chores.

I couldn't articulate it then, but if I could go back in time, I'd yell at them, "Excuse me, but I'm having a *childhood* over here."

*****

Apparently, I hadn't been wrong to dread menarche; the period I had dreaded and tried to stave off with prayers to God had proved even worse than I could have imagined, and thus began twenty-five years of sheer agony, including a series of hospital visits that finally resulted in a diagnosis of severe endometriosis. Adding insult to injury, many of the hormonal treatments for endometriosis that I endured made me feel worse. They made me gain weight—and although I was doing better with a once-difficult eating disorder, filling out against my wishes was traumatic for me. The hormones made me depressed. They gave me deep underground zits in unreachable places where I didn't even know I had oil glands, like inside my ears. Worst of all, the treatments didn't work. I was still in terrible pain, bleeding erratically, either too often or too infrequently.

*****

I didn't think my condition could get worse, but in midlife, it did.

Allow me to pause for a second to wonder aloud what constitutes "midlife." Does it begin in your mid-thirties? Your forties? How do any of us know when we are in the middle of our lives, anyway, given that we don't know when our lives will end? I think of myself as in midlife now, at fifty-seven, but how can that be, unless I live to 114? People in their early sixties pitch me pieces for *Oldster Magazine*, referring to themselves as being in midlife. As someone who has difficulty adhering to the strictures of what you're supposed to do at any given phase of life, I suppose I shouldn't nitpick, but the parameters of midlife are difficult to pin down—increasingly so as humans live longer. In any case...

Beginning in my mid-thirties, in the late '90s, my cycle somehow regulated itself, but I would cramp in varying degrees for fifteen days per month, bleeding for ten to twelve of those. I'd also experience migraines mid-month, from one to four days at a time. I don't know how I managed to work in offices, which I did on and off, much preferring to freelance from my East Village tenement, where no one else could witness me lying in the dark, doubled over in agony, and where I could do my murder scene–level hemorrhaging in the privacy of my own bathroom.

Doctors and friends suggested that pregnancy would be good for me. It would stop the bleeding for nine months, giving my endometriosis adhesions time to dry up and my pelvis time to heal. They cautioned me that in my mid-thirties, I was running out of time.

But I was unpartnered, and I was not drawn in the least to motherhood, which made me self-conscious, once again, about being offtrack. What was wrong with me, I wondered, that I wasn't naturally inclined to want to embark on that next phase of life? It wasn't unlike my resistance to getting my period as a tween and teen. I wanted to remain unencumbered and carefree. I wanted to still hang on to my girlhood. Midlife, as I saw it playing out around me—people getting married, having kids, leaving the city for the suburbs, taking lucrative jobs they hated so they could afford a more bougie lifestyle—didn't hold much appeal. Above all, motherhood looked to me like a trap.

What I didn't yet know was that in addition to endometriosis, I also had adenomyosis, a similar condition in which the muscular walls of the uterus are corrupted by endometrial tissue, which causes it to violently cramp, as mine did. My uterus was effectively Swiss cheese and would never be able to carry a baby to term. (I had two unviable pregnancies in my thirties, and two abortions to terminate them. Each time I felt nothing but relief.) I'd find all that out in my early forties, when I was newly remarried to a very boyish second husband I'm still happily married to, and trying, against both our true natures, yielding to cultural pressure, to make a baby.

I'd need a hysterectomy. At forty-three, it would turn out to be one of the best things to ever happen to me, not only because it resolved twenty-five years of unbearable pain and hemorrhaging, but because it also set me free from an expectation imposed on me, both externally and internally. The husband—now in his sixties and still delightfully boyish—would be equally pleased with this turn of events. We'd be free to live the creative life we both prefer, working by day, tending to our writing and music and other artistic pursuits by night, in a big, run-down house upstate that we've come to think of as our "arts camp."

I was relieved to have a medical excuse not to have to become a mom, but also mad at myself for not simply knowing I could choose to opt out—that I shouldn't have needed a doctor's note. And I was relieved to say goodbye to the period I'd never wanted, the bloody "curse" I'd begged God to help me avoid, which turned out to be *so much worse* than I'd ever imagined. (I was reminded of the Orthodox Jewish men who pray every morning, thanking God for not making them women.)

With that operation I bypassed a major phase of midlife: I shot straight from my childbearing years to menopause. And yet I somehow felt *younger*. While my peers were parenting small children, then teenagers, then young adults, and more recently becoming grandparents, I was in one way a crone, but in another way, returned to a version of my resting state:

girlhood, this time with arthritis and wrinkles and gray hair and a mortgage, but still, unencumbered, girlish me.

All my life I've been fascinated with a certain kind of woman, in whom you can always observe the little girl at the root of her, no matter her age. Patti Smith. Ina May Gaskin. Ruth Gordon. Growing up, some part of me knew I'd like to someday join their ranks. Now I'd like to think that maybe I have.

*****

Here I am, once again off-track from everyone else, but happily so. It's the same for me with midlife—or late midlife, or early old age, or whatever you call the phase of life you're in at fifty-seven—as it was with the onset of young womanhood. I'm not doing what so many of my peers are, and that's fine with me.

That said, living "off-script," as I refer to it, can sometimes cause anxiety. There are times when it's hard to connect with friends and relatives who are living more conventionally. There are junctures in life where I'm not sure what I'm meant to do next. And things could really get dicey later, when Brian and I are older; being childless also means having no kids to care for us later.

But for better and worse, it appears as if I might be life-stage agnostic. This agnosticism and uncertainty, and endless childlike wonder about what it means to travel through time in a human body led me to start *Oldster Magazine* so that I could examine this phenomenon, not only through my own weird experience, but through the experiences of others as well.

One thing I keep coming back to is that the greater part of me at eleven and thirty-five and forty-three and fifty-seven, and probably every age after, is at heart, naturally...a girl.

CHAPTER 5

Never Too Late

On Midlife Reinvention

We cannot become who we want to be by remaining who we are.
—Max De Pree

Sometimes It Simmers

TONYA PARKER

I had just returned home from NYC weary and a little groggy, but my insides still reverberated with the light buzz that comes when you let yourself get swept up into a fast-moving, vibrant city. I had just seen *Tina: The Tina Turner Musical* and been mesmerized by the young woman (the understudy) who managed to fully embody the electrifying icon on stage—the one who reinvented herself in midlife as a rock 'n' roll superstar.

I had booked my trip a few months back in the hope of seeing Adrienne Warren—the young actress who won a Tony Award for portraying Tina, a rising star bursting with talent who hailed from my hometown. Her mother and my husband, George, had been in the same PhD program, and I watched her beam with pride as we raised our glasses to her at the cramped bar of our local watering hole.

I remember balancing on the stools, my feet not quite touching the floor, on a dreary evening the November before. I was with George and four others, including the proud mother who had gone through the same doctoral cohort. As the only cohort outsider, I perched on the stool watching their hands flail about as they told story after story of yesteryear. They roared with laughter before even finishing whatever it was that you had to have been there to understand. Occasionally I'd be asked to snap a picture of the jubilant group from my position on the outside. But I was pulled right into the fold when the subject of Adrienne starring as Tina rolled around.

"Tonya loves musicals," George said, draping his arm around my shoulder and nudging me toward the group. It was true. I'd fallen in love with Broadway in my twenties, taken not only by the talent on the stage but by the discipline and the tenaciousness that kept them there. There was something steadfast and dependable about Broadway—the show would always go on. After the happy hour reunion, I quickly added *Tina: The Tina Turner Musical* to my must-see list, and early the next spring I embarked on the trip to Manhattan to do just that.

I wasn't alone as I sat in the theater with my own cohort of sorts—a group of midlife women with whom I shared both a love for the big wide world of the arts and our tight-knit local community. Our bodies nestled closely against each other in seats that seemed to be made for small children or perhaps full-grown people from a different time. We made ourselves small, but our hearts swelled as we watched Tina both overcome and become. After the show, we spilled out onto the sidewalk electrified as we allowed both our bodies and our minds to expand. If Tina could do all of that, what else might we do?

Unbeknownst to me that would be my last trip anywhere, besides the occasional search for necessities, for an entire year. After getting comfortable at home that night, I tapped open my Facebook page and saw a friend posting what seemed like a dog whistle. She was known for posting recipes or carefully curated photos of her kids, but her post was frantic and seemed out of character. "THIS IS MORE THAN THE FLU," she'd written. I'd heard a few rumblings, so I tentatively clicked on her distressing post, and what followed would take me down a rabbit hole about an unknown virus that was making its way through the city I'd just returned home from.

The buzz would grow louder over the next few weeks, and we'd soon learn that it was bigger than the Big Apple. The virus was spreading its tentacles and beginning to touch cities across the country. But the city I had grown to love had begun to take a beating. *New Yorkers are tough*, I told myself. *It will all be over soon.* But then, on March 12, 2020, Broadway closed its massive doors, and I knew we were all in trouble.

Days turned into weeks, and everything slowed to a snail's pace—everything except my work as a midlife influencer. Without expensive photo shoots to rely on for their images, the brands that I worked with reached out for photos I could safely shoot from the comfort of my home or on nearby empty streets. My followers were also more engaged. People seemed to gravitate to their online communities, and I too felt joy from our interactions there. But as our real worlds turned inward and we experienced more of the same routine—scrolling through social media or binge-watching the newest show—the air started to feel thick and stale. I looked for a window. I wanted to usher in something new while still being able to maintain the perceived safety of my bubble.

I thought about journaling. I had also been contemplating telling my story about the death of my father and how it led me to take the leap into the world of social media influencing, but I never had the time before. Now, I had nothing but time. As someone immersed in academia—a full-time school counselor and former adjunct community college instructor—becoming an influencer seemed an unlikely trajectory. But here I was, and in the last two years I'd had more new experiences as an influencer than I'd had my entire life. There had to be something there. Was there a story? If so, maybe it would help someone else take the risk and throw their hat into the ring of midlife reinvention one day.

"What about a writing class?" George suggested. I mulled that over for a day or so and then began researching online classes. A local writing center was now offering classes via Zoom. I browsed until a daytime memoir class caught my eye. Over the next year I'd dip in and out of writing classes, working on my craft and, more importantly, connecting with many other midlife writers who were also in transition.

One day I grew tired of my writing—not the act itself, but the memoir I had started to piece together.

"I have an idea," I said to my older daughter on the phone one afternoon. "What if I turned my story into a novel?" I asked with trepidation in my voice. Instead of inspiring others to act with a memoir that was starting to feel like a how-to, I simply wanted to write the book that I wanted to read.

"I love that," she said.

Later that night I had a few *who do you think you are?* thoughts emerge, but I swatted them away. While I had always been a reader of all genres, as a writer I had only written nonfiction. Was I trying to become a novelist with fifty knocking at my door because I was....dare I say it...bored? That didn't make any sense to me. I'd just gone through a pretty risky reinvention placing my master's degree on the shelf while I entered a field that was proverbially young and typically blond. I'd carved out a space for myself in an industry that wasn't made for me. I was proud of my success there, so why was I shape-shifting again so soon?

I believed that reinvention during midlife came on suddenly, stopping us in our tracks like walking into a wall. We'd rub our pounding foreheads and change direction. The experience would be painful—a contentious divorce, getting fired from a job you'd had for years, or, like in my case, the sudden loss of a loved one. Those things happen to most of us at some point in our lives. And more often than not, they uproot us, spurring some sort of instantaneous shift. But changing course the way I did didn't happen at all in the way that I imagined it would.

It came to me quietly. I allowed myself to become a writer in my forties. I shift in my seat as I type those words. The word *writer* still feels elusive and subjective—aren't we all writers?

The truth is I wrote a self-help book long before I believed I was a writer. I was in my thirties and a single mother then and listened as friends encouraged me to write a book. "Tell us how you do it. How do you manage it all so well?" So I wrote a self-help book for other single mothers and put it up on Amazon so that my friends and family members could access it. It was fun and easy to write, but I didn't put my whole self into it. I didn't expose the messy parts. For example, I talked about my penchant for healthy eating and exercise, but I didn't share about my traumatic health scare that inspired that change. I didn't consciously leave it out. I just didn't realize that true writing was like turning yourself inside out.

When I think back to the first thing I wrote where I accidentally did just that, I realize now what a pivotal moment it was for me. I was sitting in my high school psychology class when my teacher leaned against his desk, the metal legs scraping against the linoleum. He reached into a pile and pulled out an essay about dreams. His tone was measured as he read not about a dream but about a recurring nightmare—the one about my childhood home ablaze. It had haunted me for years.

"The flames flicker before my eyes…You're just not responsible," my teacher read, in a tone meant to mimic the last words that were said to me by the firefighter on the scene. He reread my last line twice more with emphasis, then looked up. His rheumy eyes met mine. I slid my back down the plastic chair, my cheeks burning. He went on to explain to the class why the essay was, in his opinion, so poignant, but my eyes stayed glued to my desk. I could feel my heartbeat in my ears as my heart thumped louder. Later that night there was a stirring in my chest.

Did that stirring mean that the fifteen-year-old version of me wanted to become a writer? Of course not. She decided that day, perhaps because her psychology teacher had seen something in her, that she wanted to be a psychology major. She did, however, understand that writing had a quiet kind of power—the power to make me and maybe even others feel something. I don't think that fifteen-year old me understood the what or why behind that feeling, but I can recall that moment vividly, because inside of her there ignited a tiny spark.

When I look back on it now, I want to grab my younger self by her slender shoulders and pull her close to me. "Why didn't you want to write?" I'd whisper. "You must have realized that it was hearing your words read aloud and knowing that they'd resonated with another human, not the psychology class itself," I'd implore, begging her to go deeper and think bigger. But the truth is I already know her answer—she'd never even fathomed the idea that writing could be a career.

Writing was a hobby in my parents' eyes, and my real love—reading—was an even more leisurely one. As a kid, I devoured book after book from our local library, sometimes reading under a tented Holly Hobbie comforter by flashlight for fear that it would be ripped away. My mother couldn't understand why I wasted so much time with my nose in a book. My leisurely reading obsession seemed to enrage her. And I lived in a world where little black girls and boys were reminded by their middle-class parents that they had to be "twice as good to get half as much," and reading for pleasure was not part of that equation. So I surmised, maybe even unconsciously, that writing wasn't either.

Though I didn't embrace writing passionately in my young adult life, it was always there for me like a quiet ember. I would fan the flames when I needed it, writing letters—often complaints against some perceived injustice. My emails burned right through the recipient's inbox, employing them to respond right away. My friends and family members started asking me to pen their letters too. My writing made me feel powerful again. I used it like a sword—pulling it out on a whim and then tucking it away.

In midlife, I grew more confident in my writing because I needed to. I never imagined that I would become a novelist, but that small flicker I felt in my sophomore year of high school only grew stronger. I know now that the thing I longed to do always longed for me too. The whole process of writing requires that you expose your underbelly, and if you're really on a writing tear, you'll do that thing where you turn yourself inside out. All of that quiet time of introspection during quarantine made me want to do just that.

It's been three years since I signed up for that writing class, and I've just finished the manuscript for my debut novel—the one I put my whole heart into. I now know that reinvention doesn't always come in with a roar. And it doesn't always upend your life. I'm still an influencer, but I'm also a writer—a word that I'm learning to "wear" now. I drape it across my shoulders and slide my arms through the holes. It still feels a little too big, but I'm growing a little each day.

I've reinvented myself again, but my second midlife reinvention wasn't swift or forced; it was a slow burn. It took over thirty years to ignite. A friend confessed over coffee one morning that she despised all of this "find your passion" talk that the celebrity-style gurus were doling out, because nothing had shaken her up and screamed *this is it!* I sat for a moment watching her sip her coffee as her eyes flitted around the room. I wondered if, while she was busy looking for the big thing, something small might be stewing inside her too.

"Reinvention doesn't always boil over. Sometimes it simmers," I finally replied.

The Midlife Itchies: A Self-Reinvention Story

DR. SARAH MILKEN

My parents haven't been gone for five minutes when the sounds erupt: *pop, hiss, pffft.* Each noise ricochets in my eardrums. This is one of my husband's many quirks: He must deflate every balloon that has dared take up space in our house the minute a gathering is over, no matter if it's Father's Day brunch or—as it is today—my birthday. *Pop!* Another balloon deflates, and the shiny golden *P* that was part of the "HAPPY 45TH SARAH" arch display mere minutes ago droops down to the kitchen floor (I ordered it; my husband thinks balloons are overpriced). The party was f***kin' over.

But I wasn't too sad to see my decorations go. What was I truly celebrating? Here I was, just turning forty-five years old. After getting an Ivy League education and a PhD in educational psychology, I chose to be a "stay-at-home mom," whatever that means these days. At times I'd like to call myself a "desperate housewife" without the facelift (don't worry; it's scheduled). But now, the routines that had defined my life were beginning to unravel. My kids were fourteen and sixteen; I would soon have to face a reality that wasn't defined by carpool lanes and baseball games and help with after-school homework, or at least supervising it getting done. Teen Daughter said I don't know anything past second-grade math. My husband was a fantastic partner but one who had a fulfilling career outside of the home. He wasn't worried about his "meaning" and was a f***kin' hobbyist—piano, tennis, golf, house A/V programming, and dog walking, not to mention his affinity for sports cars that would sometimes just appear in our driveway.

The week leading up to the big day, I started itching all over. I couldn't trace it back to any rash or mole, or any other weirdo skin thing that had started popping up over the past few years. I thought maybe it was my vagina, which had been suffering from frequent perimenopausal UTIs—or "yeast beasts." But while the vaginal estrogen satisfied *that* burn, the other itch wasn't satisfied. The more I itched, the more I realized this wouldn't go away no matter what cream or medicine I bought and slathered all over myself. It was a diagnosis only I could arrive at by dusting off my eighteen-year-old PhD. I was experiencing a severe case of the "midlife itchies"—a common condition that runs rampant in midlife women who are seeking to get out of the routines that have defined their lives thus far to find some novelty and self-reinvention. OK, so I finally knew what the f**k was going on. How to find a cure?

After leaving the mess of the kitchen for my OCD husband, the "dishwasher supervisor," to deal with the next day, and with Teen Son and Teen Daughter having returned to their favorite corners of the house, I decide nobody will notice if I go back to the fridge to satisfy a midlife craving. Reaching for a spoon to scoop one more dollop of cream cheese frosting from the cake, I hear it—not the pop of the balloon but, this time, a crinkle. I look down to see a golden flash stuck to my shoe, the leftover wrapping paper from Teen Daughter's gift to me. Inspired by a post on Pinterest, she had created a box filled to the brim with confetti and tootsie rolls and—most importantly—notes from everyone in my life, from my BFFs to my parents to the family dog, all responding to the question "What are three things you love about Sarah Milken?" I hadn't had the chance to read through all of them when I opened the box; I probably registered that they were thoughtful and loving (this was done before the huge puberty surge, when Teen Daughter was still nice to me).

Inspired, I take the box from the kitchen counter, kick our family golden retriever out of the spot that he and I negotiated over (slobbered with his saliva, of course), and take the time to open, read, and absorb every note that had been written about me. They start off sweet and hilarious and wonderful enough:

—Heart of gold

—Reliable, trustworthy, there when you need her; can find humor in anything

—Loves family beyond words

—World's best pharmacist; she brings an entire drugstore on our family vacations

But as I read through each golden letter, I started to notice a pattern emerging...

—She's my pretty nerd friend

—She's my curator

—She's my information gatherer

—Always lets me know that I'm not alone in the roller coaster-y world of West Side parenting

—Straight shooter

—Walking Rolodex and ready to help anyone

—Always call Sarah for unbiased advice on any situation

And my favorite:

*—She's my friend who would pick me up after a
3 a.m. emergency call with a full face of makeup*

I didn't know what any of this meant. Yet. All I knew was that the next morning I realized I hadn't itched the entire night. This golden box—and the notes contained within—was onto something. It had created a midlife stir, a sense that change could happen. That it wasn't too late to start something new.

"So I'm a good mom. A good friend. Apparently, a frustrated pharmacist. What next?" I asked my frentor (friend/mentor) on a neighborhood walk the next day. My frentor was five years ahead of me in the midlife journey and had become a trusted resource for me to vent and chat about all things WTF, including: WTF was this hair, WTF was this mood swing, WTF was this life. The Los Angeles sun (cue the derm, the plastic surgeon, the melasma specialist) was beating down on us as we made our loop, me wearing my Teen-Daughter-not-approved "mom visor," with a splash of boob sweat on the side. "You're not giving yourself enough credit. That box means something, and you have to find out what."

"How?"

My frentor slowed her pace, looked me dead in the eye, and uttered the words every midlife Angeleno woman hears when walking around her neighborhood: "Hire a life coach."

So I did. (I didn't know what the f**k a life coach did until my frentor suggested one. Apparently, a life coach is like a therapist who helps you set goals rather than tell you what to do. I could get into that.) Cari was a warm blanket for a raw midlife nervous system. Whereas I constantly judged myself as if I were trying on bathing suits under a harsh department store light—nothing fits, nothing works, why am I putting myself through this, I should disappear forever—Cari would constantly reassure me that I *got this*. I loved her vibe immediately.

She thought like I did, in extended metaphors, and understood my glossary of newly added midlife language. My birthday box was the treasure trove containing all the daily midlife affirmation I needed to make myself feel better so that I could get to the real golden nuggets—the real work—of what I was supposed to be doing in midlife. It wasn't just that I was known and seen and loved by those around me for the qualities that I brought to the table. It was that I was in charge of *setting* the goddamn table, filling the spaces around me with everyone from my husband and kids to a pussy yoga instructor, a woo woo psychic medium, and a midlife nutritionist who "allowed carbs" and told me that perhaps cardio wasn't the end-all be-all. I was the *Encyclopedia Midlife-tannia*, if Google had a sassy midlife BFF. Not only were my phone calls to friends and doctor (and psychic) recommendations valuable to those around me—they had the potential to be valuable to other midlife women too. I should take my curious mind and unfiltered TMI mouth and curate an onslaught of midlife experts to explore topics from midlife pivots to empty nests to vagina rejuvenation. I should start a podcast.

But where the f**k was I going to start? And how? My teenagers called my attempts at relating to them "cringe." I was a social media virgin. I had zero followers. Could I learn the technology? Could my brain stretch that f**king far? *I can't get out* *of my own way*, I kept repeating. My inner bitch was screaming, "You can't sit with us." The external peanut gallery was yelling, "Who do you think you are? A midlife woman talking about her midlife vintage vagina that is in desperate need of a reinvention and full lube job." What I didn't know at the time was that I was in the midst of my own midlife crisis, one I have irreverently coined my "midlife remix." It was hard and sweaty work.

To compound the difficulty of embarking on a new venture, two weeks after I started, the pandemic hit. I remember the first time someone Zoomed me; she was gobsmacked that I answered the call in a full face of makeup. At the end of our conversation, she asked me why I felt the need to dress up when I was lounging and stuck at home. My first lesson, my first mantra escaped my lips before I could even think about it for half a second: "Because I do it for me." The woman smiled. "I'm not judging you for not wearing makeup," I said. "You do you, I'll do me. Everyone has to pick their own lanes." The woman loved that. Smiled, hung up. I stared at my glittery face in the Zoom box: I could do this. I wasn't too old. It wasn't too late.

Every day after that, I woke up, slapped on a full face of makeup, and got to *work*.

I took over a corner of my bedroom and claimed it as my home office. Teen Son set up my microphone. I put my golden birthday box on my desk, a reminder of why in the hell I thought I could do any of this.

First, I would need a name. I wanted the title to draw on the duality of my midlife experience: Though on the outside I look like I have my shit together, on the inside I'm constantly ruminating. "She's so chill!" My teens' friends will often tell them. "Yeah, wait till the door closes," they reply. Thus, *The Flexible Neurotic* was born.

My frentor agreed to be my first guest.

I started posting on Instagram. My husband hated it, so I started affectionately calling him "Instagram Husband" on the podcast.

I lost entire days to writing and rewriting while talking back to the inner bitch in my head, telling her to shut the f**k up. The days of high school were over. I didn't need any more mean girls in my life.

I got a few hundred followers.

I got a one-star rating.

I made another episode. Then another.

I took more walks with frentor and Cari. Packed my crossbody fanny pack with wipes, mini waters. Tissues for hike pees. The crossbody was supposedly "cooler," but Teen Daughter still didn't approve.

I got three positive reviews.

I made another episode. Then another.

I hadn't itched in weeks.

Two and a half years later, I find myself asked to write an essay about my self-reinvention. My Instagram has ballooned (see what I did there?) to 55.5 thousand followers. My podcast has a 4.9/5–star rating, with 337 reviews. One woman said I interrupted too much. LOL! Duh! Listeners from across the country commend me on the "midlife realness!!!!" and "information goldmine" that my episodes deliver.

I head up the stairs to my office (my exercise for the day). On my desk sits a box, the gold-leaf wrapping paper curled on the edges. The tootsie rolls are unopened and hard. (Gross.) The notes are just as wonderful, kind, hysterical, and necessary as they were when I first read them two and a half years ago.

But they're more than that too. Those notes are the reason I picked up my (actual and metaphorical) golden shit shovel—which would eventually become a symbol of my platform—and started digging through the layers of my own midlife shit to get to my midlife remix. They're the reason I created a second act that is as equally meaningful as my first.

Beyond the followers I've acquired, the listeners I've amassed, and the content I've created, those notes are the reason I got up the day after I turned forty-five and chose ME—and made the hard choice *not* to cancel on myself. Again and again and again.

I haven't itched since.

I Wasn't Always a Butterfly

SUSAN KANOFF

*Reinvention: The action or process through which something
is changed so much that it appears to be entirely new.*
—Oxford Language

My husband calls me a butterfly because he has witnessed my transformation. I am stronger and more powerful now at sixty-one than I was when I was young. I've broken out of my cocoon, spread my wings, and flown into new territories.

But I wasn't always a butterfly.

My early story may sound familiar to some. The negative messages and traumas from my past annihilated my self-confidence and self-esteem. Fear of failure, or even of succeeding, held me back and prevented me from pushing my limits and discovering all the amazing things that I'm capable of accomplishing. However, I truly believe that our life experiences build muscle, making us stronger and wiser as we get older.

A long time ago there lived a woman with thick layers of trauma in her life. She had zero self-esteem, was afraid to speak her mind, and tried to please everyone. On the outside she seemed happy, but on the inside, she was miserable. She felt awkward, "less than," and her self-esteem was in the toilet. That was me.

I was an unhappy child—a ball of anxiety and self-loathing. When I was young, I suffered from severe separation anxiety and frequently made an early exit from school or friends' homes because of "stomach aches." I was afraid to try new things and dropped activities as quickly as I signed up for them. Although I had friends, I felt different from them—invisible, unlovable, and ugly. I desperately wanted to fit in, but my insecurities made it impossible for me to feel accepted.

Fast forward to college—I attended University of Massachusetts Amherst, where I partied up a storm, skipped classes, and focused on winning attention from boys. But I hit rock bottom, when on the first evening of my sophomore year, I was brutally attacked on campus. Although I recovered from the physical injuries, the emotional trauma took a toll on my fragile state of mind, knocking my self-esteem down another notch. Feeling like damaged goods, I made bad choices, on some level hoping that I would self-destruct. Looking back, it's a wonder that I graduated *cum laude* with a degree in social work and made it out alive. It's ironic that I thought I could counsel others when my own life was in shambles.

When a marriage proposal came my way at the tender age of twenty-one, I jumped at the opportunity. This would be a new beginning for me. He said that he loved me, his family adored me, and it would be a chance to start a family of my own. It felt like a real shot at love. But I think I knew from the get-go that we probably weren't right for each other; I was just too young and naive to fully recognize it. For fourteen years I stayed married to the wrong person, hoping that I could fix things. No blame goes to him; we just were not a good match.

The marriage was fragile and explosive at the same time. We were different people with different needs. I cleaned, cooked, managed the finances, and took care of the kids and my husband. I tried hard to be the "perfect" wife, but I was miserable and felt stuck in a situation that at the time I didn't know how to leave. We tried marriage counseling, but it was an epic failure.

There are times in life when we can choose to sink or swim. And I decided to swim hard even though the current was against me. My unhappiness boiled over, and I had no choice but to call it quits. I felt like I was dying inside. So, I left the marriage with two young, emotionally distraught kids in tow.

If you've ever been through a divorce, you probably know that most of them aren't pretty, and mine was no exception. I went from being a wife to a single mom, supporting my children on a few hundred dollars a week in child support that I supplemented with a small income from a part-time social work job. My kids were devastated over the divorce and all the resulting changes to their young lives, including moving from a home they loved into a small condo in an unfamiliar neighborhood. I spent many sleepless nights consoling and reassuring them that everything would be OK, though truthfully I wasn't sure it would be. I pinched pennies to make ends meet and lived in therapists' offices.

As bad as my situation was, leaving an unhealthy marriage was the first step to rediscovering myself—for when we get unstuck, we unleash our power and true potential. We learn that we can fly.

Four years after my divorce finally went through and after years of battling it out in court, I married Richard, a dad of two. Although blended families come with their own set of issues, we were able to work through them as a team. Richard fully supported my hopes and dreams and respected my boundaries, something that was entirely new to me. I had never felt so unconditionally loved in my whole life. He encouraged me to pursue my passions, and when I told him that I wanted to start a side gig as a wardrobe stylist, he was on board even though I had zero experience in fashion other than a love of clothes. I made some business cards and held my breath, but unsurprisingly, the negative messages came flowing back into my head. Who would want to hire me? I didn't know Valentino from Gucci, and I felt like an imposter. I was shocked that clients quickly booked sessions and loved my services. One thing led to another, and before I knew it, I was styling several Boston television personalities and had a robust clientele. The more I accomplished, the more I believed in myself and wanted to do even more.

During this time, I also took on additional hours at work. I ran the Family Self-Sufficiency Program, a HUD-funded initiative to move low-income families out of poverty, and accepted a role as the co-facilitator of a statewide group of social service professionals. An important component of this position was public speaking, my worst nightmare! In the beginning, I struggled. I remember once speaking in front of fifty people and losing my train of thought—I was horrified that I froze and had to be rescued by my colleague. But I brushed off my bruised ego and did it again and again and again. And after a while, I became pretty good at it. My confidence soared, and I took on more work projects and created new initiatives. I even won state and national awards for program innovation! Who, me?

Confidence builds confidence, and I became a bolder version of myself.

My styling clients asked if I could show them how to put together looks on social media. My tech skills were pathetic, but I taught myself and created an account called *The Midlife Fashionista* on Instagram and Facebook. I also launched a blog under the same name and started posting style and beauty tips. In retrospect, my selfies were, shall we say, less than high quality, and my outfits weren't great either, but the accounts started to grow organically. People told me they liked that I was real, relatable, and authentic, and I quickly gained followers and friends. Although I wasn't planning to become an "influencer," that's exactly what happened. Clothes, shoes, accessories, and beauty products arrived, and I got offers to do paid posts. Over the years, I've worked with many well-known brands, such as Clinique, Chico's, and Eileen Fisher, to name just a few. One brand sent me to collection launches in NYC, where I was treated like a celebrity and seated at dinner with actress Tracee Ellis Ross, creative director Adam Glassman, and fashion magazine editor Lesley Jane Seymour. And my daughter and I were chosen to be the faces of a Soma Intimates Mother's Day campaign and whisked away to Florida for an amazing photoshoot!

Then everything came full circle, and I found my true purpose. My styling clients wanted to know where they could donate their clothes directly to women in need, so I started a "closet" in my social work office to assist the women I worked with. When one of my clients needed clothes for work, a job interview, or just as a pick-me-up, I would put together beautiful outfits for her. This continued for years until my director submitted the "closet" for a state award, and to my surprise, it actually won.

I was lucky to have a director who believed in me. Cathy encouraged me to turn the closet into a program of its own.

I had dreamed about this for years, but how could I make it happen?

Enter Uncommon Threads, a nonprofit organization in Lawrence, Massachusetts, that empowers women in need through fashion and personal development coaching.

As a mother of two, a wife, a social worker, and a wardrobe stylist, I was pretty darn busy, so the idea of starting a nonprofit of my own was daunting. I reached out to a friend—the CEO of a large nonprofit organization in my area—to see if she would be willing to take the program under her wing as a fiscal sponsor. I thought it would be a long shot, but she said yes right away. It was a great fit for her program and made launching Uncommon Threads a lot easier for me.

All the stars were aligning, but I needed money to get Uncommon Threads off the ground. I started selling some of my clothes at consignment shops and on social media to get seed money to launch. A dear relative gave me a generous gift for a new home we were about to move into, but instead I donated it for start-up expenses. I also did some local fundraising to pay for a small space and some basic supplies. I reached out to my social media community for clothing donations, and they came in fast and furious along with amazing volunteers, some of whom would become lifelong friends. For the first six months, I held down two jobs in addition to working countless hours at Uncommon Threads. It was grueling, but rewarding and satisfying at the same time. When you follow your passion, work doesn't feel like work.

Uncommon Threads is now an established and highly regarded program that has served close to ten thousand women in need over the years. The program is unlike others in that there is no employment requirement to access services. Instead, the mission is all about building self-esteem and self-confidence. We can dress a woman for job interviews, style a mom for her child's school meeting or a grandmother for her grandchild's birthday party—all with dignity and respect.

Social media has been a powerful tool for getting the word out about Uncommon Threads, and through connections made there we just launched a second chapter on the West Coast. It's also been an amazing vehicle for clothing and monetary donations. Through *The Midlife Fashionista*, I've been able to bring on big-name donation partners who have fallen in love with the program.

This may all sound too good to be true, but because life is life, there were bumps along the way.

In 2018, I was diagnosed with chronic lymphocytic leukemia (CLL), an incurable but treatable type of leukemia. It took me by surprise. I felt fine but had a few swollen lymph nodes that my doctors chalked up as my body fighting an infection. Finally, blood work confirmed that I had cancer.

Although I was told that I probably wouldn't need treatment for a long time, if at all, four years later my leukemia heated up. In the fall of 2022, I started a yearlong treatment consisting of a combination of infusions and oral chemo.

Enter COVID, which posed a huge risk to me in my immunocompromised state. I spent three years of my life living like a hermit, unable to physically go to Uncommon Threads. Because I couldn't be there, I hired a program director to manage operations and started working remotely. To keep me safe, my husband also started working at home, and we stopped going to large events, restaurants, movies, and more. Even getting together with others was difficult to coordinate. When life felt almost impossible, my family and friends pulled me through.

Because I was so isolated, I joined an online CLL support group and was surprised that one of the moderators, Michele Nadeem-Baker, was a woman my age who lived about thirty minutes away. I stalked her on LinkedIn, and we chatted on the phone like old friends. The friendship blossomed, not only because of our shared cancer but also because we had so many other things in common. We talked about the need for a CLL support group specifically for women around our age and for an online community to bring hope to women impacted by cancer. Together we created CLL Women Strong and Kicking Cancer in Heels.

Reinvention requires digging deep into your strengths, passions, and life experiences to create your next adventure. As I write this, I feel proud of myself for all that I've accomplished at age sixty-one. My life has been hard, but each struggle and hurdle has made me more resilient and resourceful. My past wounds have transformed me into a stronger version of myself—a woman who feels capable and confident.

CHAPTER 6

The Pleasure Principle

Reigniting the Senses

Something in her was violently sensual, alive, earthy.
—Anaïs Nin

Please Please Me

LAURA FRIEDMAN WILLIAMS

It is past 2 a.m. on a cool spring night and I am in the PTA office at my kids' elementary school. I am standing behind the desk, still zipped into the gauzy black dress I donned eight hours ago for the school auction, my feet now happily settled into flip-flops. I am the PTA president and I take my job seriously; it is the only job I have known since deciding a decade ago to stay home with my kids.

A team of us diehards are here in the wee hours of the night, unloading items from the gala that did not get picked up. We are almost done, giddy at the success of the event but also bone-tired, the last effects of the copious Prosecco we drank having worn off in the U-Haul truck. We are thanking the dad who performed the manly duty of driving and unloading the truck. He is cute: tall and scruffy with a British accent that has all the moms here swooning.

He says goodbye and turns to leave, but then does an about-face.

"There's one thing I have to do before I leave," he says, swiftly marching around the moms and the desk and planting a kiss firmly on my lips. It is the most passionate kiss I've received in two decades since first hooking up with my college sweetheart, whom I would go on to marry. He is gone before I even understand what happened.

The room erupts in nervous and confused laughter and we carry on. A few hours later, makeup scrubbed and messy hair pulled into a ponytail for school drop-off, I bump into the dad outside school.

"Can we pretend that didn't happen? I'm sorry, I don't know what got into me," he says. I blush and nod my head, but I wonder—had I sent off some kind of signal that would have led him to be so bold? And did I wish for more?

I am in my late thirties and will go on to flirt with men who are not my husband. I am not wholly aware I am doing it, but I am very aware of the benign crushes I have: on the swarthy twenty-something guy who inherited the pizza place on the corner, whose gaze I hold when I order a slice for my son every afternoon after school; on the Adonis who sells fruit and weed on the beach in the Caribbean whose eyes I can feel burning into me as I saunter down the beach with my kids and husband; on the barrel-chested dad with whom I wile away blazing afternoons at the local pool while our spouses work and we mind the kids.

I desire these men but less in a physical way than an emotional one—though I certainly find them physically appealing, it is their attention I crave as I see myself through their eyes: not as a harried and underappreciated mom but as a vibrant woman who deserves a second look.

Years later, my husband is no longer an impediment to my finding out what happens when flirting takes a foothold in reality and not just fantasy. I am forty-seven, and I am neither single nor married. My husband has had an affair and I do not want him back, but I don't want to be without him either. I am a woman in transition: no longer ripe and young, but not quite past my expiration date either; committed to the idea of my marriage more than the reality of it; a mother to two children who are soon to fly from the nest but another so young she is missing her front teeth. I am neither here nor there, teetering in the middle where any step can take me back to where I was or forward to the great unknown; I may yet find my best self or, terrifyingly, pray for a return to the self that turns out to have been the best one if I am lucky enough to find her.

I edge my way forward, planning baby steps: First, try to look beautiful. This is no easy task. I feel dead inside; putting on lipstick and mascara will only result in presenting me as a corpse ready for her unveiling. I try to use other senses and land on smell. I slather French rose body oil on my skin and the scent is subtle but rich, not overpowering but soft and mellow. I tend to the rest of myself as best I can, letting my curls dry naturally, dabbing concealer on the deep purple underlines of my eyes. I do not need a man to find me and passionately kiss me—I need to be seen; I need to know I am not a ghost. *I am still here*, I want to shout to anyone who may hear me: rejected and humbled, aging and uncertain, but here, I am here.

I take myself out on the town. I am a city girl but I am in the country for the summer, and town is a small, quiet affair with limited options. I make a deal with myself: one drink and then I can crawl back into my burrow. I walk into a bar on a Saturday night alone. I take it in: the couples leaning intimately toward each other, groups of friends throwing their heads back in laughter. I feel alone in the most primal, aching way. I am not just unaccompanied in a room full of people who are together; I am lonesome and forsaken. If there had ever been a time during my marriage when I fantasized about having a one-night hall pass, this was not what it looked like. That notion had been illicit and exhilarating; this is a sorrowful house of mirrors in which every angle shows me in my unattached state as a woeful and abandoned creature.

I realize with sudden alacrity that anything that happens or doesn't happen from this moment on is up to me. No one can save me: not my beloved friends or my supportive mother or my husband who is about to be no more. Either I choose to go forward, or I choose to go back; this state of purgatory can only last so long. I am on my own. Scariest of all, I will have to own whatever I choose.

As has been the case in many pivotal moments in my life, I am driven by two parallel desires: one, to live, to really live, not simply coast through my life; two, to do whatever I have to do not to feel regret later. If I don't try, I won't know, and right now I have a burning need to know. Who am I beneath the surface, what can I be aside from a wife and a mother? All those years when sex was limited to the safety of my marital bed, I engaged in it because it was expected of me. I had a waning interest in sex over the years, but I didn't miss it, what it had been when it was fun and carefree, what it had been before it became an occupation—first to get pregnant, then to satisfy my husband. I had traded a vibrant sex life for motherhood and what had been, for a long time, a happy marriage. But now, being single, I am going to date again, and dating means sex, not to make babies or keep my husband placated but simply for the sake of feeling another body against my own, for the purpose of making me feel full and sated: pleasure for no other sake than pleasure itself.

Amidst the small groups gathered around the long mahogany bar, I spot a man. I sense, right away, that he is the one. No woman in sight, no wedding band on his finger. There is something in his jaunty manner and easy laugh that catches my attention. I stare, openly and without self-consciousness—after all, I am unseeable, and a ghost can do as she pleases. He makes his way next to me; I find my voice. I do what I think I am supposed to do as we chat: smile until my dimples deepen, shrug my shoulders suggestively, shake my curls until he tells me that my hair smells good. After an hour of this, I know that I need more. I want him to see me naked; I want the warmth of our bare bodies to merge. I want to feel physically tethered to him and, by extension, to this world.

I invite myself to his hotel room, and there, while he uses the bathroom, I shed my clothes. I will be seen, I will be touched, I will be inhaled. I want it all, all that has been forbidden to me in the past twenty-seven years, all that I convinced myself didn't matter to me anymore. He enters me and I think, *So this is it; I am almost fifty and losing my virginity for the second time in my life.*

I was sixteen the first time and didn't know I was allowed to want to feel sexual pleasure, didn't think sex was for me as much as it was for him. I was thirty-eight and kissed by a veritable stranger and felt like a giggling, shy teenager again; any desires that ignited in me I immediately shut down so I could continue to live satisfactorily in the life I had created. Now, here in midlife, softer around the edges, my body having done the job I most wanted it to do, producing three babies who stretched my skin and sucked milk from my breasts until they sagged, in bed with a man I have known for mere hours, I feel alive.

He says words that I repeat as if I am learning a new language: *pussy, cock, f**k.* I feel his tongue on my clitoris, I put his penis in my mouth. I feel it all, every lick, flicker, touch, and thrust. I have never been f**ked before, of that I am suddenly certain, and my body is both succumbing to it and demanding more. I orgasm and instead of feeling sated, I want another.

Lying back against him as we catch our breaths, I run my index finger along the edges of the tattoo on his shoulder. "You're going to be OK," he says, and I cannot manage a response. This man has beheld me in all my vulnerability and power and has affirmed for me what I have believed only to the most infinitesimal degree: I will one day emerge from the chaos swirling inside of me, and I will be OK.

I drive away, back home, a dull ache between my legs and a grain of hope in the calmness of my breath, back to the sleigh bed I shared for so many years with my husband and whichever child found their way between us during the night. I put my hand over my heart, my patch of pubic hair, the curve of my hips, my breasts that spill to the sides of my body. I am far from the withered shell of a woman I have believed myself to be, nearing her sell-by date. This body is mine; it has only ever belonged to me. I let people use it all these years, boyfriends and my husband and my kids, but I am reclaiming it now to satisfy the desires I thought were long gone, if they ever even existed.

Yes, I think, *I am going to be OK; I am already finding my way.*

Midlife Awakening: Finding My Way Back to Pleasure

GABRIELLA ESPINOSA

Sex was never spoken about in my family. The only "talk" I ever received was from my grandmother, a devout Catholic who immigrated to Queens, New York, in the 1960s from her native country of Ecuador, and it came in the form of a warning: "Your body is a temple, respect it, and don't let anyone in!"

Yet sexual expression in its many forms was all around me, and I was acutely aware that sexuality was a natural manifestation of being female. During festivities and gatherings, the women in my family could dress provocatively, plunging necklines, bare backs, and high skirts. They moved sensually, their hips swaying to wanting melodies. There were playful suggestive comments. Externally, billboards of Brooke Shields and nothing coming between her and her Calvins, and the femme fatales in Hollywood movies, demonstrated the same. Yet these expressions of being "female" were at odds with the messages I received as I moved into womanhood. I was told to "be a nice girl, don't dress that way, don't touch yourself there, don't be a whore, save yourself for marriage," and, the closing argument to any admonishment, "what are people going to think!" I sensed an intense fear all around me over accessing knowledge that would bring me closer to my true sexual nature.

As women, many of us are conditioned to believe that sex is shameful or dirty, and as a result, unhealthy narratives shape the way we think about our bodies and our desires. Add to this conditioning the inadequate sex education we received—which focused on abstinence to avoid pregnancy and STIs—the pressure to have babies to define your worth, and women's magazine headlines touting, "50 ways to please your man," and it's no surprise that I reached midlife blissfully ignorant about what it meant to be a sovereign sexual being.

The entirety of my sexual experiences—and the sense of myself as a sexual woman—was exclusively wrapped up in surrendering myself to a man. I believed that this was the only way to experience pleasure. Thoughts of self-pleasure, when they somehow managed to surface, felt foreign, taboo, and I felt embarrassed to even consider it.

That is, until perimenopause swooped into my life unannounced, around my forty-second birthday. It was as if someone flipped the light switch on my libido, leaving me in total darkness. The fiery, can't-take-my-hands-off-of-you honeymoon phase with my husband was over, and I felt utterly disconnected. I didn't have the language or understanding to communicate to him what was happening inside me. This manifested in awkward body language, slight bristling when he would come up behind me and nuzzle his face against the nape of my neck, and in quickly getting dressed after showering to avoid giving him what now felt like the wrong message.

My husband adored me, and I wanted to want him back, but I felt dead inside. Night after night, I lay in bed pretending to be asleep or making excuses like I wasn't feeling well. On the nights I did say yes, it was often out of a sense of duty, even though my body was silently screaming *no*. I would go through the motions, forfeiting my own climax because I couldn't muster the energy to care. I was the dutiful wife, prioritizing his pleasure over my own. Afterward, I would lie awake, staring at the ceiling, asking myself, "Is this it? Is my sex life over? Am I getting old?" Deep inside, a sense of shame gnawed at me—my pleasure no longer seemed to matter.

One day, after another loveless night, I stood in front of the mirror and asked myself, "Who am I as a sexual being?" I was knee-deep in motherhood and sleepless nights, organizing playdates, music lessons, and sports matches while striving to be the perfect mom and wife. It was fun but exhausting, and there was no room left for the sexual self I once knew. I had exiled her—she didn't fit the cookie-baking, soccer-mom mold I was desperately trying to squeeze into. Yet from somewhere deep inside, my inner voice made its way through the cacophony of life and whispered, telling me to take pleasure into my own hands. I looked down at those hands, delicate and feminine yet strong, and in that moment I knew they were capable of taking me to places I had never previously gone. I decided to embark on a self-pleasure practice—a journey of rediscovering my body and what truly lights me up.

Through self-touch, I began to explore parts of myself I had long ignored, reclaiming the pleasure that had always been there, just for me. I had to start somewhere, so I began by looking in the mirror again—but this time I was looking intimately at my vulva, learning her shapes and colors, naming all the different parts, and seeing her beauty for perhaps the first time. I was finally befriending her, and together, we explored different types of touch—I stroked and massaged her, found out what kinds of touch—and where—were most sensitive and pleasurable, and discovered how she responded when I focused my attention there. My hands mapped out an infinite terrain of clitoral nerve endings and discovered a whole new alphabet of pleasure zones, including the elusive G-spot. I mapped out my body's pleasure anatomy and became a detective, finding clues that led to discovering new parts of myself. Through this process I learned that self-pleasure wasn't just about sexual gratification—it was about connecting with my entire body, and about loving myself. More than just my genitals, it was about creating new neural pathways that allowed me to understand what turned me on and, more importantly, what didn't. I could finally own my pleasure, something I had given away for far too long. Self-pleasure became a beautiful act of self-love—a way to come back to myself, to appreciate my body as it was, not as I thought it should be. There was no right or wrong way to do it. It was a personal exploration, and with every touch, I peeled back layers of stress, numbness, and disconnection that had built up over the years.

Interestingly, the deeper I went into this exploration, the more I started to ask myself more generally, "What do I desire?" This question, though simple, was one I had never really considered. So, I sat down and made a list, answering that question beyond the context of my bedroom, thinking more broadly about my life as well. It was the beginning of reclaiming not just my sexual self but my entire being. This knowledge wasn't just freeing; it was empowering.

One day, feeling more confident than I had in years, I took my husband's hand and asked him to sit with me. I told him I needed to share something that felt vulnerable but incredibly important. I told him how much I loved him, and how I wanted things between us to be even better. With a deep breath, I shared my deepest desires—more slowness, more tenderness, more time. I explained the secrets of female pleasure, the anatomy I had discovered, and what truly lit me up. He listened with wide eyes and a curious smile and said he was eager to join me in that exploration into desire and pleasure.

That conversation changed *everything*. Together, we began redefining what sexual pleasure meant for us in midlife. Sometimes it looked like luxuriating in each other's presence as he watched me self-pleasure, or allowing him to take the lead in offering me the kind of touch that transported me into ecstatic states of arousal that did not necessarily involve penetration or the goal of orgasm. Other times our erotic energy would naturally lead us into waves of orgasmic bliss. One thing was certain—I was no longer giving my pleasure away. I had taken it back, and I wasn't letting it go.

During this journey of self-discovery, I realized that in at least one sense my grandmother was right—my body *is* a temple. It is a temple where I get to worship through my self-devotion and where I make choices about whom I invite to join me there, and when they are welcome to come in. And I learned it wasn't the hottest tips, tricks, or toys that would help me reclaim my sexual self, but rather getting to know myself intimately, peeling back the layers of shame, and disproving the stories that said I was not worthy of pleasure. I finally welcomed my sexual self home.

Midlife, as it turns out, isn't the end of my sexual journey—it's a new and exciting chapter. Self-pleasure has become a pathway for my own awakening. Now, five years postmenopausal, I feel more at home in my skin than ever before. I accept and appreciate my body and recognize myself as a sensual and sexual being who owns her pleasure, her power, and her purpose. I've learned to lovingly communicate my authentic desires—to myself and others.

I am finally and fully awake and alive!

CHAPTER 7

Mirror, Mirror, on the Wall

On Midlife Beauty

Youth is a gift of nature, but age is a work of art.
—Stanislaw Jerzy Lec

All Day I Wonder Briefly

SKYLAR LIBERTY ROSE

It's an hour after waking and two cups of tea before I properly look at myself in the mirror. I clean my teeth and ponder my reflection. The light in the bathroom is soft, but not soft enough to disguise the skin under my chin, which is slack and sagging. It occurs to me that I have jowls now.

A memory tugs my mind back to another place, a different face, and there's a jolt of something I can't quite pinpoint as I recall my twenty-something self and how she invariably found something to criticize about her appearance too. As always, I'm surprised not to see her reflected back at me. I have no idea where she went or when she left. I only know that I am forty-nine years old, and I have become my grandmother.

I wonder briefly whether a lottery win would see me at the surgeon's office having a no-commitment consultation, a mere conversation, about possibly tucking this or potentially smoothing that. But even if I did opt for a cosmetic procedure, where would it end? If they took care of my face, then what about my neck? What about the crinkled skin at the tops of my arms, the crepe texture that covers my thighs, the stretched-out skin I see on my breasts whenever I lean forward?

I leave the bathroom and walk into my home office, stepping onto my already rolled-out yoga mat. A few minutes later

I'm in downward dog, and as I glance at my legs, I see how gravity is clutching at my entire body, pulling me down into an ugly spiral of self-doubt, and I wonder briefly if there are any kind angles left.

They say your body is never the same after having a child. But I have not had a child. And I wonder briefly if I get to forgive my body in the same way that mothers do as they mourn what was once tight, shapely, and smooth but smile as they shrug any regret away—because look (look!) what they have to show for it. Look at the life they've created. I have committed the cardinal sin of occupying an aging body without having anything to show for it. What's my excuse?

At my desk, I prepare for a Zoom call and use the video preview to check my appearance. I'm sitting in front of the window, but there's also a window behind me, and the light isn't as flattering as I want it to be. I turn on the ring light and I wonder briefly what the life expectancy of this magical device is and whether it might die on me mid-call, taking my airbrushed-esque glow with it.

I have never considered myself to be beautiful according to societal standards. My nose is too big, my ankles are too thick, and for years I longed to have the smooth, straight, shiny hair that all the pretty girls at school were blessed with, instead of unruly curls that would never lie flat no matter how much heat and hairspray I used. Still, I spent my teens and twenties devouring all the magazine articles and soaking up all the dos and don'ts, trying to make the best I could with what I had. I utilized makeup and fashion to help bridge the gap between me and beautiful, and on a good day I could pass for being the right side of acceptable.

But I've never been able to shake off the feeling that my painstaking efforts are all so flimsy. My attractiveness has always been dependent on how cool my outfit looks or how meticulously my makeup is applied. Take away the enhancements, and the illusion comes swiftly tumbling down, exposing me for being utterly average. And now I am aging. Now there is less to work with and more to improve. My proximity to beauty is becoming more distant by the day, and since it's the only currency I've ever been taught matters, I wonder briefly what my worth is now.

As I wait for the meeting to begin, I realize that it's almost the two-year anniversary of the emergency craniotomy I had to remove a benign tumor—a tumor that wreaked havoc on my body, causing fluid to build up in my brain so that I was constantly vomiting. I'm pulled back into another memory, this time of returning home from the hospital unable to walk unaided but still using all my might to shuffle from the walker onto the bathroom scale, because despite knowing that weighing myself is as good for my self-esteem as reliving the memory of my mother calling me a fat pig when I was sixteen, there was still a thrill of joy when I saw how low the number was.

Later, I take the train into the city. The inspector passes through and checks my ticket. She looks to be a few years older than me, and I want to ask her if she's ever felt truly beautiful in her body, or if her flaws are always at the front of her mind too. Instead I smile as she thanks me and wishes me a good day.

As I stare out of the train window, I wonder briefly what it would be like to peel my clothes off in the middle of Manhattan and stand in the crowded street with my arms flung wide open, letting my sagging, stretch-marked body be seen in all its terrible glory. The body I have always been told to conceal and cover up. The body that was too distracting for teenage boys, then too tempting for grown men. The body that is now too old to be either a distraction or a temptation and is simply an abomination because it's dared to decline. The body that has been sexualized, objectified, and now vilified.

I think of the paradox of what it is to have donated decades of my energy seeking approval from a patriarchal culture that never truly saw me, only to feel more confident in many ways knowing now that at almost half a century old, I am barely seen at all. But then I wonder if it is in fact confidence, or if it's that I simply stopped caring. Being bound by rigid societal rules has become less interesting to me as I get older. Still, it is hard to break away from the conditioning completely.

On 34th Street, I walk into the beauty store, and out of the corner of my eye I see the young greeter glance in my direction and then go straight back to looking at her phone. She does not welcome me to the store, but a couple of seconds later I hear her greet another customer who looks more like the models in the posters on the walls. I wonder briefly if at her age I would have seen me either. How many times did I walk past women who look like me? How many times did I ignore the woman I have become?

I head to Central Park to meet a new friend, and we walk and talk as the winter sun warms our faces. When she takes out her phone to snap a selfie of us, I think of all the times I've sucked in my stomach for photographs or not permitted myself to smile fully in case I highlight my crooked teeth. And yet I have not saved the world by being less of myself. Nothing wonderful has ever sprung from my shame.

On the train ride home, I scroll on my phone and see a headline that femicide is rising globally. A few moments later I see an advertisement for a skin cream that promises to reduce wrinkles, and I wonder briefly why aging offends us more than violence or death.

The light outside is fading, and I marvel at how quickly a day can disappear. I think of all the brief moments that become months and then years, and I wonder whether there's ever been twenty-four consecutive hours in any decade when I've felt a complete sense of ease about my appearance.

At home, I wipe off my makeup, and I stare in the mirror to see how time has marked my skin with memories my mind has forgotten. My body is a map of everything I've experienced and endured, everything I continue to survive. I send out a silent apology to all the women I've been before, the women I've punished for being too much or not enough. I feel them each exhale in gratitude.

Mysterious Charge

LAURA BELGRAY

I asked my husband, Steven, to go through our latest Amex charges because I can't deal. I instantly regretted it. I had a window to say, "Never mind, I'll do it." If I weren't allergic to being financially responsible, that's what I would have done to avoid fielding questions about the shockingly high payment I had cheerfully said OK to at the dermatologist.

One of the office women, Stephanie, writes the amount you owe on a piece of paper. She folds it and hands it to you from behind the desk, like on TV when they slide a number across the table in a diner booth. I've never understood that. Sometimes it's a salary offer, sometimes an extortion sum that you have to pay by midnight in a duffel of unmarked bills. Why don't they just say the number out loud?

In the exam room, the medical assistant, also a Stephanie (everyone in the office is Stephanie) sets things up. She snaps photos of my face from all sides with an iPad, reminding me not to smile or pose. It's a struggle to resist because I'm too vain to let a camera catch my face in repose. I don't have resting bitch face so much as resting jowly-mouth-breather-with-turkey-neck face.

Next, she hands me the iPad and has me sign a waiver. I've never read it. I'm sure it says something to the effect of "I acknowledge that whatever we're about to do could FUBAR my face and make me wish I'd left well enough alone when at least I didn't look like some cosmetically disfigured D-lister in those sponsored clickbait posts: 'You'll never guess what this once-famous loser looks like now!'"

After I fingernail scribble my signature on the iPad screen, Stephanie asks if I need a headband to keep my hair off my face before she spackles on the numbing cream. I always accept one and then wear it out still on my head, half-accidentally but not. I'm probably supposed to give it back, but what does it cost, a dollar? And I'm paying so many thousands.

How many, I don't want to know—any more than I want my husband to. (So far, he hasn't mentioned it.) I've mentally done some loose math. It's not pretty. Not pretty what it costs to stay pretty after fifty. Money and pain.

I almost like the pain? I think the more it hurts, the better it must be working. The doctor gives me squishy neon stress balls, which quickly grow slimy with my palm sweat. I breathe like a woman in labor while she applies the hot, pulsing torture machine and make her dish on who's had what done. "All the Jennifers," I pant through clenched teeth. "Tell me."

She thinks Aniston's overdone it with the threading. JLo has "done it all," she asserts, but you can't discount good ol' genetics. Garner, we didn't get to. I keep meaning to circle back on that. She looks like one of the naturally lucky ones. But maybe that's just great work?

Instead of all this, couldn't I radically accept myself? Embrace my aging? Give the "zero f**ks" we're supposed to possess after fifty? Agree that if you're alive, you're "aging well"? Theoretically, sure. In reality, I'm still married to the idea of looking younger than I am. Of revealing my age and getting an astonished *GET THE F**K OUT!* Suddenly, in this decade of my life, I've been getting an unsurprised nod—as if to say, "Fifty-something, that tracks." *How dare you?*

I hate that I'm so ageist. I blame Instagram. Any time a female celebrity of a certain age posts a selfie, the comments range from "What's your skincare routine? We need it!" (if she looks fresh and youthful) to "Wow! She's aging so gracefully!" (if she's Paulina Porizkova) to "She got old lol" (if she's daring to sport jowls and wrinkles) to "She should sue her plastic surgeon! I wish she'd let herself age gracefully" (poor Madonna). By the way, we all know "aging gracefully" means looking sculpted and miraculously unchanged, except maybe rocking silver hair.

Whenever I'm off to an appointment, I tell my husband I'm "going to the dermatologist." Not a lie. He knows I'm "doing stuff" and that I sometimes come home with what looks like a bad sunburn. "Are you disfigured?" he asks, peeking through his fingers. I tell him it'll fade in a couple of hours, which it does. I assure him it's just lasers and promise I'm never going to be one of those Botox victims on Bravo whose frozen foreheads seem to be sliding down to their tits. And I swear up and down that I'll never get lip filler. Our friends, a male couple, got his-and-his injections and looked for months like they were wearing those wax lips from the Halloween store.

I do get Botox in my neck. That's the first thing the doctor did to reduce the jowls—or, as my friend Vic called them, my "problem." I liked thinking no one but me noticed. But of course she did, even if her neck and jawline are as tight as a twenty-year-old's, so she has no reason to fixate on everyone else's like I do. She only gets worry lines on her forehead—a no-brainer fix with a touch of Botox, although one botched treatment did leave her asymmetrical, with a single Spock eyebrow. "Luckily, Jason hasn't noticed," she said. "He has no idea I get Botox, and

I'll never tell him so you can't tell Steven." Meanwhile, Jason texts Steven rows of laughing emoji about the idea that she thinks her Botox is secret. "Don't tell her Jason knows," Steven said. He and Jason hate that stuff and have always called full makeup "clown face." Or, if it's right to my (clown) face, Steven will say, "Oh, you've got Lady Eyes on."

I never told him I'd gotten a tiny shot of Botox above my lip. It smooths out the fine lines but also gives you what's called a "lip flip." I did this when I'd gone in three or four times for my Problem. Fix that, I thought, and I'll be happy. Yet now, somehow, I'm one of those women who say, "What else could I be doing?" I see how it happens! This doctor is conservative and will never suggest anything I don't inquire about. She's not like that dentist I once went to for a cleaning. He said, "You know, I could fix that crooked front tooth with veneers."

All the same, if I ask, "How about this area, any way to bring back the fullness?" she'll happily break out the syringe. She was pretty sure my upper lip wouldn't bruise, but it did because I bruise like a peach. Only one sharp-eyed friend seemed to notice. "You have something right here," she said, reaching to wipe it as I stopped her. "Oh, it's a bruise. From lasers." For some reason, I'm fine talking about the lasers but ashamed of saying "Botox." Botox is no more vain than lasers but for the last decade, I've bragged, "Nope, never done Botox," and strangely don't want to admit that I now have. As for Vic, she now maintains that she knows Jason knows, but he doesn't really know. "I haven't had Botox in six months, but he thinks I just did it. He's so dumb about it."

So is it working, my "laser journey"? My jawline does look straighter. I think the under-skin has tightened a tad, but I can't help scrolling reviews for a product all over my feed called

Crepe Erase. I wonder if I'd even think about this body region if Nora Ephron hadn't pointed it out with the titular essay of her book *I Feel Bad About My Neck*. No, I'm sure I'd get there all on my own. When I pull back that skin in the mirror—like a stylist clipping a boxy shirt in the back—I look twenty years younger. Would it be that complicated for a surgeon to snip and stitch it like that? My search history is full of variations on "neck lift without full facelift before-and-afters." I don't want the whole megillah. Hard no to whatever Ellen and my friend's mother have had done that removes all the under-sag but leaves you looking like your head is a potato on a stick.

Even if there is a simple nip and tuck, though, I end up wondering, "To what end?" Would it fix my life? Would it make me that much more confident and successful, and even if so, is it worth going under the knife? I think of Kanye's mom. Joan Rivers. What if I died from a surgery Steven would never want me to have in the first place? What a terrible thing to do to him.

But I can't stop obsessing. I have for years, even when my neck sag was barely in its budding stage. A fifty-something woman I met during my forties had a serious wattle. She called it "scrotum neck," which struck me as horrifically accurate.

After the first treatment, I started taking daily photos of my face from underneath. Scrotum-neck selfies. You know, to track the progress. It became a weird tic on my walks. Open camera app, snap ghastly pic. I then tap the three dots at the top, select "Hide," and the image goes into iPhoto's hidden album. I suppose most people use that destination for nudes and dick pics. It requires a password or face ID to open, which is good because I'd rather die or end up on a porn site than have someone—especially my husband—stumble on a gallery of my neck scrotum, even if it's become minimally less dangling. Uncounted thousands of dollars later, it'd better be. If Steven notices on the bill, I'll tell him it's all for sun damage. That sounds kind of medical, right? Almost like a mammogram. Don't worry about that charge; it's health-related stuff.

Empowered Beauty

LAURA GELLER

There's something so beautiful about the way our faces tell a story. Every little line, every little crease, evidence of a life lived—the laughter, the tears, the smiles, the worries—it's all there. Which is why I find that women often become even more beautiful with age, and why in 2021 my brand shifted to featuring women over forty in our marketing and advertising—something that was completely unheard in the youth-obsessed beauty industry. But I wanted to highlight real women who had lived, women who were defined not by their age but by their experience and wisdom. Women who had become even more beautiful with the passage of time, and women who, despite what society might tell them, still have a right to look and feel good.

I have always believed that if you look good on the outside, you'll feel good on the inside. It's the philosophy I built my entire business on. I've seen countless women—at every age—completely transformed by the simple act of putting on makeup.

As it is for many of us, my mother was my first point of reference for so many things in life. She was never the most fashion-forward woman and rarely wore makeup on a day-to-day basis. As a homemaker, her focus was always on our family. But I was an observant child, and I noticed that whenever she *did* take out her makeup bag, she *transformed.* She became more confident, she held her head a little higher, and it was so apparent that she felt great.

Growing up, I noticed it with many of the other women in our neighborhood too. There was a marked difference in their confidence levels when you saw them wearing makeup. It went beyond the way they looked; it was all about how they *carried* themselves.

I became transfixed with makeup and the way it could empower. Whenever I had special occasions as a teenager—my sweet sixteen, my prom—a family friend in the neighborhood would always help me with my hair and makeup. I loved it, and the way it made me feel, but it wasn't until I graduated high school that I saw it as a potential career.

Shortly before I was to go off to college, I ran into a classmate. "Where are you going to college?" I asked. She wasn't. Her plan was to go to beauty school to become a hairstylist. I was surprised—she was one of the smartest students in our class. "Why don't you join me in beauty school?" she asked. Intrigued, I met with the owner of the school, who promised me I would be very successful in the business. "You have a good gift of gab!" he said. I had no idea how right he would ultimately be.

Fortunately, my parents were very supportive of my decision to pursue a career in beauty; I graduated with my cosmetology license within a year and quickly took a job at a major beauty brand, where I was lucky to find my first mentor in the business.

Initially, I focused on the aesthetic side of the industry—mostly facials and spa treatments—and did a little bit of makeup work every now and then. But when I started to study theater and film makeup on the side, everything changed. The class focused on face structure in a way that almost made it feel like a science. I went in expecting to learn how to apply the perfect eyeshadow on an actress; instead, I was learning about anatomy—the structure of the cheek and jaw, the proper way to measure eyes and lips, and how proportions factored in. I learned the art of it all in an entirely different way, and ultimately, I understood what I wanted to do with my life. My goal was to teach women how to apply makeup for one (very important) reason: *to feel their very best.*

For ten years, I worked in a makeup studio in New York and had gigs doing TV and theater makeup as well. My chair played host to some of the most glamorous celebrities in the world—Lauren Bacall, Audrey Hepburn, and Ginger Rogers, just to name a few. But my favorite clients were the real, everyday women. Watching them come alive, seeing their whole persona change while they were in my chair—that's what I lived for. They would hold their chins higher; they would dare to look at themselves in the mirror. It brought me tremendous satisfaction to play a part in changing the way they saw themselves.

Connecting with my clients in this way led to the birth of Laura Geller Beauty; they loved the education that I provided, and often they would want to buy the products I used on them so that they could recreate the look (and that feeling) at home. I realized then that I could create something special—products of my own that I would use to educate women and help them see their true beauty. I opened up my own Laura Geller makeup studio on the Upper East Side of New York in 1993, complete with my own branded products. In 1997, I made my first appearance on QVC. Twenty-seven years (and a lot of life) later, mine is the longest-running color cosmetics brand to be featured on the network.

My life, like anyone else's, didn't come without hardship and dark times. My parents divorced when I was very young, and I had to figure a lot of things out on my own. Maybe the biggest lesson I learned as a young person was the importance of being a strong, independent woman—one who could always find a way to take care of herself. And that meant persevering through the many ups and downs on this ride. I was not an overnight success; in fact, my brand didn't become nationally known until I sold a majority stake in my mid-fifties. And while at the time I found myself wishing it had happened sooner, I realize now that it was right on time. At fifty-five, I was self-assured and had the confidence to see to it that the philosophy and integrity of my company was maintained. Ultimately, what kept me going through all of it was the fact that I was doing something I loved.

Above all, what I've learned over the years is that it's *never* too late. I'm in my mid-sixties now and don't feel any older than I did when I was just starting out. Recently, I was named one of QVC's Quintessential 50 on its Age of Possibility platform, featuring fifty-plus women who embody the idea that this chapter is full of possibility and opportunity. I was also honored to appear on the Forbes 50 Over 50 list, which highlights that age and experience can be our best assets, and proves, as Forbes puts it, that "there is no deadline for becoming who you are meant to be." Many of the women on these lists did not hit their stride until they reached their fifties.

I'm still practicing my craft and doing the work I love. In recent years, I've had folks ask me when I plan to retire. "It's time to stop and smell the roses," they say. But I've been smelling them all along. I don't have another hobby—my work is my passion. I read about new makeup innovations and new trends in the industry daily. And I'm still connecting with a new generation of women every day, showing them through our forty-plus campaigns that age is not something to fear. That it brings richness, texture, and beautiful new dimensions. That each line tells a beautiful story.

I guess you could say, I'm *always* looking ahead.

CHAPTER 8

Facing the Inevitable

On Love and Loss

*You are never stronger than when you
land on the other side of despair.*
—*Zadie Smith*

Flying Motherless

DINA ARONSON

I was twenty-one years old and standing in the Publix Danish Bakery in Gainesville, Florida, the first time I learned my mother had cancer. I can still remember the sweet scent of all those pastries juxtaposed with the sour sound of those three little words she reluctantly uttered. Never one to steal the spotlight, she hadn't planned to tell me until after my college graduation that weekend. But from the moment she and my father arrived, I could tell something was off.

That's how it always was with us. Deep, instinctive knowing.

She probably thought she could wing it and maybe even forget about her new reality for a day or two while she celebrated her only daughter, the one who was rewriting the story, the one who took it to heart when she said repeatedly over the years, "You must always be able to take care of yourself; you must always be independent." As the daughter of an Italian immigrant mother, higher education was not part of her cultural lexicon, but she made damn sure it was part of mine.

We made it through that first dinner, my parents borrowing from the *Freaky Friday* script. Dad, usually reserved in social situations, was downright animated, while Mom was uncharacteristically quiet, participating in conversations but not fully there. Comic relief came in the form of an overwhelmed waiter who was sweating profusely and kept returning to the table without our food to tell us the delay was due to nonspecific "problems in the kitchen," which left us all speculating wildly as to what was happening back there, and half expecting a disgruntled line cook to bound out swinging a butcher's knife. I'm pretty sure she laughed with us, but she was not herself, and after some end-of-night badgering from me, she went off to the hotel, her secret still intact.

Being the future litigator and pain in the ass I was at twenty-one (a trait my husband would argue has stuck), I continued my direct examination the next day. "Why are you acting so weird?" "What's going on?" "Something is wrong, why aren't you telling me?" G*d, I was annoying. This went on for a while as we went about preparing for the day, which is how we found ourselves standing in the bakery, picking up goodies to enjoy over the weekend. It was there that I broke the witness. "I have cancer," she blurted out, there among the rows of freshly baked breads and colorful cookies and all manner of pastry. The words fell out of her mouth and into my ears, and though quietly spoken, the sound of them was deafening. I have no recollection of what was said next. I just remember feeling scared, and as I was wont to do at the time, catapulting myself to the worst-case scenario—life without my mom. It was unimaginable to me at twenty-one.

It remained unimaginable until it actually happened, thirty-three years later.

*****

I am on a plane, flying motherless at the age of fifty-six on what is the second anniversary of her passing. As I look out the window and into the clouds, I'm transported to my brother's bedroom in my childhood home, the one with the window that looked out onto our circular driveway. It was there I would watch for her to come home from work, and in some ways, looking out this tiny airplane window, I'm watching for her still.

She was fifty-one when first diagnosed with breast cancer in 1990, a time when there was no internet and no easy access to research or answers; luckily, one of my brothers was dating a health reporter on our local NBC affiliate, and through her network we were able to find an excellent oncology team. I remember sitting in the surgeon's office after her lumpectomy/lymph node resection, classical music playing, listening to him describe the procedure. "The tumor was larger than we thought; I wouldn't be surprised if the cancer has spread." There it was, that worst case scenario, the one I would live with for the next ten-plus days, the amount of time it took to get pathology results back then. When the call finally came telling us the lymph nodes were clear, I saw my father cry for the first and only time in my life.

We didn't really talk about death and dying when I was growing up, although I sensed that my mom, present and mindful before the advent of meditation apps and self-help gurus, was not afraid in the same way that I was then, and in the way I remained through much of my adult life. In the first grade, Sister Christine, for reasons I have never figured out, talked to a class of six-year-olds about what happens when we die. "The worms crawl in, the worms crawl out," she said, describing our eventual return to the earth. I remember coming home and asking my mom if I could be buried with her, my six-year-old brain not grasping the absurdity of this question. I couldn't imagine being without her while those worms did their thing.

It wasn't the worms I was afraid of at twenty-one, but I still feared death (and so many other things), and the idea of losing my mom terrified me. She had been my person. My rock. A source of pure, unconditional love, a love that powered me and provided the fuel I needed to believe in myself. She was also my co-conspirator as we worked around my father and his well-intended but overprotective tendencies. She was a lover of life and wanted me to experience it fully and freely. She pushed me to go, to see, and to do. I often wonder how different my life would have been had she left me back then. Despite my maturity and old-soul status, I don't think I would have been emotionally equipped to process or manage the loss.

At fifty-six, it's still a struggle.

*****

I was home for Thanksgiving, sitting on a hotel lounge chair with my mom when the call came. The irritation on her breast, the one she thought might have been caused by her new bra, turned out to be something else. The cancer was back, twenty-two years later, or perhaps it never left, instead slowly and quietly growing, evading the biannual mammograms and ultrasounds, until it found its way out. Sitting there with her, taking in the news, was like traveling back in time to that bakery—I was twenty-one all over again, feeling scared and powerless.

But I had also lived a lot since then, and my (forty-three-year-old) instincts ultimately kicked in. I didn't yet grasp or accept that I have very little control over most of what happens in life, and I sprang into action, determined to fix it. My mother would not die on my watch.

Truthfully, despite my hard wiring for rational thought, when it came to my mom I was fully subscribed to some serious magical thinking. Not only would she not die on my watch, she would not die. Period. I held on to this crazy fantasy until about seventy-two hours before she actually did just that, passing peacefully into the night, ready and on her own terms, eleven years after that second call came.

There were many ups and downs through those years, but the one constant was gratitude—gratitude that she had lived and was healthy for decades after the first diagnosis, and gratitude that she was able to manage well through the next round. No matter what was going on in her life, she was always able to find a way to it, and when she died, it was gratitude that kept me afloat when I thought I might drown in sorrow. I continue to hold on to it like my life depends on it, and in many ways, I think it does.

*****

In some ironic sense, facing the thing I was most afraid of helped me to let go of fear. When the worst happens, the world as you know it may change, but it continues to spin; you may feel dizzy and completely disoriented, but you begin to understand in a very meaningful way that "life goes on" is more than just a trite saying. And ultimately, if you let yourself feel, if you can access that gratitude, for all that was, and for all that remains, in time you begin to find your footing again.

One of the unexpected residual effects of losing my mom has been a heightened sense of presence. It's like a deeper awareness of self in the sense of where I am and what I'm doing at any given moment, and a newfound need to truly experience it. Without thinking about the list of things to do. Without worrying about what's next. And without fear, which is actually a place I've been trying to get to for most of my life. It's a new kind of mindfulness that has opened me and has enabled me to see and feel things I might have missed before.

So even on hard, clunky days, this gift born of loss means that I can still find joy, even in the smallest of everyday things—a beautiful blooming flower, a cuddle with my kitty (whom I sadly lost as we were finalizing this book), a call from one of my stepsons, a found rock in the shape of a heart—all little ordinary bits of happiness there for the taking when my eyes and heart are open. I know now that it is possible to hold both joy and sorrow, that the two can peacefully coexist, when we allow ourselves to just be exactly where we are.

There is no getting around loss. If we are lucky enough to get older, it's an inevitability. But I've learned that it is possible to adapt and find new ways forward. To hold on to the contours of love that will always remain, but use the space left open to honor and to create. To find light through the darkness, and to continue to fly, even motherless, into worlds of new possibility.

CHAPTER 9

Midlife Friendship
Wanna Be Friends? Finding Your Glorious Broads

Some people go to priests; others to poetry; I to my friends.
—Virginia Woolf

Same Sheriff, New Posse

MARYJANE FAHEY

"I miss you. And I'm not coming back."

Shit.

Another one bites the dust.

But this ain't about dying.

These are girlfriends. Besties. Fleeing and getting the hell out of town. Basically saying, *It's been fun. It's been real. But I'm out. Bye-bye.*

It felt like the ultimate dumping by a lover—but worse.

With paramours, you know there is a fifty-fifty chance of the relationship going the long haul and actually flying—but GIRLFRIENDS—they were supposed to be with me through thick and thin. Thin won.

This was my life during COVID. At seventy, I was posse free.

I always had a tribe. It was built in—four sisters and me. It gave me a sense of (false) security—these bitches had my back! I was covered for fifty-two years, people! You don't have to search for others, unless they land in your lap; with sisters, you've got your backup gang forever. But then they started dropping like flies. Two gone, three to go (including me), and my sister who lived down the block had the nerve to move three hours away! To the country no less.

COVID edited out my friends, my sisters. (And, of course, my closets.)

I suffered. I missed them. I Zoomed.

Two years in, it began to feel OK. Different, but OK. I became more comfortable with solitude and began to enjoy spending time with myself and not needing to fill up every minute with my girlfriends. Sure, I missed my cronies; I had known many of them forever.

But I changed. My life changed. My interests changed. My work changed. I am a different woman. Maybe it was time to start the gang over—an edited version. Quality, not quantity. Open up that circle, but keep it tight. Meet a new posse as I am now, a seventy-year-old who knows what she wants with a much different inner compass than the old me.

How did I meet them, you ask? I started a platform called *Glorious Broads*—dedicated to older, smashing, unconventional broads. You don't have to start out on social media to start building your new posse, but it gave me the impetus and the guts to reach out. I pick them up—'80s style—like men back in the day. They are everywhere when you have your eyes peeled. I have no boundaries. I love it. They love it. This new circle may not have the history of my old pals, but that's exactly why it's working. It has brought a number of unexpected gems into my life, making new history that may only last a decade, a year, or five glorious months.

My new BFF is the ultimate New Yorker: eighty-four-year-old fashionista/jewelry designer/cultural wit—she's my very own Eve Arden, my personal Fran Lebowitz. She introduced me to the Carnegie Hall classical piano concerts only insiders know about. And I thought I was COOL?? She also demonstrates the perilous art of window shopping at Bergdorf's—of which she is an expert, and now, alas, so am I. We holler, we try things on, we talk politics and history—old and new. We make over-the-top brooches and bracelets and chic-gaudy baubles together. I've traded martinis for rosehip tea. Who am I?!? I no longer refer to her as my "eighty-four-year-old-friend"—now she's simply my friend, and a powerful Glorious Broad who has brought so many treasures (and chuckles) into my life.

And there's my neighborhood bud—a hundred-year-old ferocious icon—a dancer I literally picked up in my West Village market one Saturday morning. I eyed her across the lawn, thinking, *I am going to ask her out,* and approached her. The rest is history. She's a refugee and a legend in the modern dance world. And now, my vodka-drinking companion. This week we are packing her up for a yearly solo trip to Greece—to visit all her sacred temples. After giving a performance in her home country, Latvia. I mean…

I reached out to the cool-ass poet who knocked me out at a reading on the Lower East Side. And the fifty-five-year old scary wild-child punker who turned me on to the Brigadoon of bars I thought evaporated after the '70s. I punctured my hearing again for old times' sake. These two women would have intimidated me in my younger days as the Marianne Faithfull of ultimate cool, but not now. Now, I think, *Doesn't getting old rock?* I have less time on this planet and want to let in new fresh experiences that inspire, keep me laughing, and keep me learning on my last lap.

This forced edit of my old friends opened me up to new possibilities, and for that, I am grateful to the monster plague that visited us.

Last month, I got unexpectedly dumped by an old and very close friend. A misunderstanding that got way out of control—and all through texts, and worse, through messages on Instagram. A woman I have known for more than thirty-seven years.

I was angry. I was sad. But mostly, I was hurt.

After all those martinis, mega laughs, and slobbering cries, she was gone. How could she make OUR legacy history? I took the time to grieve. This was different from a phase out or a COVID edit.

This was getting dumped.

Why is it that we rebound from romantic breakups eventually but not from this? Is it because we say things to our friends that we would NEVER say to our lovers? Is it because we not only *dish*, not only soul talk, but we pour our guts out to them? And they get it.

Stewing, I found one of my favorite podcasts, *Everything is Fine*, covering this very subject—talking about the "closure" theory. That closure often ends romantic relationships, but there's not typically closure in friend dumping.

Well. I dumped and was dumped in all kinds of ways romantically. Often with no closure. So that theory was no help for mama.

But a few other life hacks were mentioned that were very useful.

Did you see that Jane Fonda viral hit on women's friendships all over IG? She talks about what she needs and what she's attracted to in a girlfriend. Jane's unapologetically drawn to women who keep her straight back even straighter. They keep her on her toes! The point is to aim high—especially as we age—with no room for just "hanging out" with friends. I loved this message.

And then I put my COVID-edit lesson to work in the context of an old, somewhat stale friendship.

If I met this woman at a party today, would I be attracted to her? Does she match who I am now, not the woman I was thirty-seven years ago when we met at a swank magazine? Would we have something to share? Would she keep me on my toes? My back straighter?

The answer was a very solid "NO."

I never called her again. I hit the unfollow button, and I breathed in deep. I was ready to let her go.

So…thank you, COVID? I never would have made such a drastic friend edit at this stage in my life. But in the harsh light of the pandemic, they edited themselves.

Here I am post-pandemic—closets cleaned, friends edited—and I'm recognizing the power of change. Letting in new friends, a smaller circle. And letting in the grim fact that I don't have as much time left here, living and breathing, as I want. That means very little time to waste. So, my new friend rules: It's not just about sharing DNA or having shared a joint at Studio 54 decades ago. Now, I have to be around people who bring me joy. Often they are Glorious Broads I have scoped out. I've widened the age range, the types, the unconventionality of their being to teach and inspire me—the me I have grown to be. I feel astonished to know a smaller quality circle, profound, hilarious women I can howl my ass off with.

CHAPTER 10

Style for the Ages

Dress to Impress (Yourself)

The key to style is learning who you are, which takes years. There's no how-to roadmap to style. It's about self-expression and, above all, attitude.
—Iris Apfel

I Am What I Wear

SUSAN SWIMMER

I've thought about clothes as long as I've thought about anything. Much has changed in my life as I've careened into my fifties, yet that hasn't changed one bit. I may not work in an office any longer, or go to lots of social events, or have the body I once had, but I'll be damned if I don't still love getting dressed.

Like lots of little girls, I used to sit on the floor of my mother's bedroom and watch her get dressed. She worked, so in the mornings she had to get both of us up and out the door. She'd get me dressed first, and then I'd eat Raisin Bran out of one of those little individual boxes-as-bowls while she readied herself. My mother sported a look I would call Boho Chic, although at the time I didn't know how to characterize it. It was all earth tones and textural fabrics: In the winter she wore lots of corduroy and tweed-y layers; in the summer months it usually involved patchwork denim and cotton T-shirts. Sometimes she tied a batik scarf on her curly head of hair, sometimes she wore leather-tooled sandals she purchased, no doubt, at a local craft fair. Often she'd finish the look with an armload of Bakelite bangles or Native American turquoise bracelets. Her style was her own: singular, artsy, saturated in color. Except for the times she went braless, I thought she was so cool. My mother seemed fearless in her individuality. She didn't look like the other mothers—most of whom wore sensible sheaths and classic blazers—she was different. And she seemed so *comfortable* in that difference, which was even more amazing. I didn't know it at the time, but that messaging was indelibly imprinted on me, and I've thought about it throughout my life.

When I was about ten, my mother took me on a trip to San Francisco to visit her only brother. I don't remember much about the trip, but I do remember going to a store and Mom buying me a three-tiered peasant skirt adorned with ricrac trim, a matching Western-style snap-front top and a necklace made with a pearl from an oyster I fished out of a tank with my bare hands. It was a look of my own creation—vaguely retro, a little bit hippie, with a pinch of cowboy—and it was definitely a departure from what the other young girls were wearing at the time (mostly bright, floral, poofy dresses). That night Mom and I went to the top of a fancy hotel, where there was a lounge-in-the-round, on a platform that rotated, slowly, clockwise. I remember vividly how that outfit made me feel: assured, dreamy, confident. I liked the muted colors, the delicate paisley print, the soft fabric, the way it all worked together. I always had suspected that clothes made you FEEL something, and in that moment, I was sure of it. If clothes could bring me so much joy that night, I knew they could bring me joy every night.

In middle school I went through a serious preppy phase. All my friends did too. It was the mid-1970s, and at that time the fashion landscape was dominated by haute pink and green. We had *The Official Preppy Handbook* to guide us, after all, and we extended the same reverence to it that one might feel about a beloved babysitter or a Bay City Roller. I bought my first Lacoste shirt, with money I saved from dog walking, and a navy blue grosgrain belt embroidered with little bright red whales. Even then I think I knew that the look wasn't quite me, but it did make me feel like I belonged to something, which in turn made me feel good. After all, I was at an age where belonging, in look more than anything else, was paramount. By the time I was in high school, the prevailing style preferences diverged. Some stayed the preppy course, but I became enamored with the *Flashdance* frenzy, so naturally I shredded my sweatshirts and paired everything with white Capezio dance shoes. That was relevant until Madonna entered the chat, and I started wearing an old, black moto jacket and an armload of rubber bracelets. My college years were a blur of baggy jeans, concert T-shirts, and the occasional Benetton rugby shirt.

In other words, if it was in the zeitgeist, it was in my closet.

After I graduated college, I started working in women's magazines (as a fashion editor), and on TV (as a correspondent). It was a slow build, but every year my fashion vocabulary (and my closet) grew and expanded. I went to sample sales, pre-sales, designer's showrooms. I indulged in fashion like a hungry person feasting at an all-you-can-eat buffet. I loved the austerity of wearing all black in structured silhouettes...and I also loved the liveliness of a wild print mix. I had access to just about everything, and I experimented relentlessly. Tulle skirts, cowboy boots, brocade and lamé. Miniskirts with heels, pajama tops with oversized trousers, vintage one-of-a-kind finds, and lots of leather. I once wore a fascinator to a birthday party, just because. There was an undeniable feeling of power in dressing with such exuberance. There was joy in the clothes, joy in the process of putting them together, and joy in feeling connected to other people who shared the same love and devotion. There was fabulousness all around me, and I was tickled to be a part of it. I felt creative and confident. I was also in the zone, fueled by a career on the inside of fashion, boosted by limitless energy and buoyed by the attributes of youth. Everything was firm and shiny and perky. It was not unusual for me to do a live television segment in a skintight architectural sheath and high heels by 7 a.m., followed by a change of clothes into skinny black pants with a blazer and a full day at my magazine office. I attended at least two, usually three evening events a week. That meant more outfit changes, lots of accessories, and even higher heels. When I think back now, I can't believe how much clothing I wore. I was in heaven.

Everything changed in my fifties: my work, my body, my energy, my mood, and my outlook. I still loved experimenting with clothes, but for the first time in my life I had to admit that certain things didn't work on me. They were too young, or too skimpy, or too deconstructed, or too boyish, or just too…bizarre. Youth can get away with a lot—middle age, not so much. It wasn't really a question of how it looked, it was a problem with how it made me feel. Costume-y is the way I'd describe it. I also started to realize that I wanted to change focus—like after years of accentuating my legs, it was time to move the attention upward, to put the emphasis on my face and mouth (where the thoughts and ideas came from). I found that wearing black, while still chic, kind of drained the color from my face. Oh, the times they were a changin'.

By fifty-three, I had decided to leave the media world I had inhabited for more than thirty years, once and for all, to start my own business. I went from dressing every day and commuting to work to wearing jeans and T-shirts in my home office. I went days on end without interacting with a single human being outside of my own apartment. At first, I was downright giddy about it. Ending all the getting dressed was freeing. And time saving! Day-old clothes, fluffy slippers, no bra (Mom was laughing from above). It felt like a palette cleanser, a reset.

Or something. NOT getting dressed made me discover a lot of clothes I owned but rarely wore. The things pushed to the back, relegated to closet Siberia for lack of interest—perfectly fine clothes, but not the stuff that styling dreams are made of. So, every day pretty much looked the same: jeans and a sweater. Then the pandemic hit, and just when I thought I'd reached bottom, stylistically speaking, I found an even less interesting sub-basement. I went from wearing jeans and sweaters to wearing...sweats. Not even the cute, chic sweat sets that became all the rage on TikTok, but rather ill-fitting, uncoordinated sweats of questionable origin. Every day. In a relatively short period of time, clothes went from dominating my thinking and stirring my creativity to barely flickering across my consciousness.

That this time corresponded to the unavoidable reality that my body was also changing was not lost on me. That pesky belly pooch. Crinkly leg skin. A bustline that was somehow getting larger and smaller at the same time (#IYKYK). On the very rare occasion that I did pull myself together (an outfit!), things just didn't fit my body the way they used to. The Marc Jacobs coat that made no fewer than a dozen trips to Europe was, suddenly, mysteriously snug. The pencil skirts that once made me feel like a badass only accentuated my thickening middle. The ankle boots I long-adored now savagely cinched my toes. *Had I been spending too many hours in Birkenstocks?* I wondered. There were dresses I could no longer zip. Like not even close.

I found the whole situation deeply depressing. Who was I? I wallowed in the despondency for longer than I'd like to admit. I tried, desperately and unsuccessfully, to wear clothes that didn't fit. And then I tried some more. And then I obsessively googled "How to Lose the Belly Fat." I thought I'd be a lot cooler about aging, and yet...

Thankfully, at some point, a switch flipped in my brain. I realized I didn't want to think about what wasn't, and instead I wanted to focus on what could be. I thought about something my friend's Aunt Rose always said: "Better it got good then it was good." I missed my clothes. I missed getting dressed; I missed that hit of dopamine that always came from creating a look; I missed feeling like *me*. I wanted it to get good again.

So I decided to make amends with my body *and* my closet. First plan of action? I started weeding stuff out. I stripped down to my skivvies and tried on everything. If it didn't fit, didn't flatter, and didn't work with my current state of being, it had to go. Out went the black Phillip Lim tuxedo pants that I had worn ten thousand times, the shrunken blazers that never failed, the brightly colored sheaths that looked great on camera, an incredible bead-encrusted skirt that danced many nights away.

So. Many. Heels. *Buh*-bye.

Before long, my floor was covered in the flotsam and jetsam that didn't make the cut, but I also found so many things I loved. Some had been forgotten in the volume of it all, and unearthing those beauties was like mining for treasure. A long, vintage Pucci skirt. Two silk Tom Ford blouses from his really good Gucci years. A slip dress with amazing lace trim, cut on the bias so it, *ahem*, naturally expands. A maxi dress in the most beautiful shade of green. A magenta coat that works in every season. A pair of wide-leg high-waisted charcoal pants. A men's tuxedo jacket, perfectly oversized, that I hadn't set eyes on in years.

I started getting dressed daily, and here's what I learned:

> *Wearing color makes me feel good.*
> *Heels have become torture chambers.*
> *When I'm comfortable, I'm more productive.*

I know how to camouflage the jiggly bits.
Too-tight clothes flatter no one.
I can layer like a boss.
Age and weight really ARE just numbers.
Clothes are a creative outlet.
Clothes make me happy.
I still love clothes.

Sometimes a picture pops up on my phone—me in some fabulous fashion-with-a-capitol-*F* outfit, taken at an extravagant work-related event—and I feel a jolt of...something. Not sadness, definitely not regret, but something akin to delighted-adjacent: delighted that I had that moment in time, a tiny bit wistful that it's in the rearview mirror, but unquestionably proud that I lived it to its fullest. It's possible it took me passing through so many different fashion phases to get me to this place, but I suspect it's more a matter of age, and perspective. My fashion choices may have evolved over the years, but my love of fashion has remained a constant. I still find it's the sandbox I most want to play in, and if that means putting on a plum suede midi skirt with a black beaded sweatshirt and layers of chunky necklaces in order to meet a friend for lunch, so be it. It makes me feel engaged, present, alive. Sometimes I pass another woman on the street, someone who is clearly equally interested in clothes, and we offer each other a knowing smile. And then there are other people who give me a puzzled look and ask me why I go to so much trouble. "How come you're so dressed *up*?" they say. I nod and shrug and usually make some self-deprecating crack about having a hot date, but I know what the truth is. The truth is, this is who I am. My authentic self. And if being authentic isn't one of the great privileges of getting older, then I don't know what is.

The Substance of Style

CHRISTINE MORRISON

Madeleine L'Engle, author of *A Wrinkle in Time*, said, "The great thing about getting older is that you don't lose all the other ages you've been."

Thank goodness for that. I will take wisdom over youth any day.

Much like the abounding ages and stages of life we've lived, it's what we have worn along the way that led us to becoming who we are today—and who we are still striving to be. We all have the clothing donation piles to prove it.

Studies have shown that the happiest ages are forty-six and fifty-six. I once thought the greatest joy was the age when you finally got a Birkin or a consistent good night's sleep. But if losing a parent at thirty, marrying the love of my life at the cusp of forty, delivering identical twin boys as a "geriatric," and pitching my first book at fifty (and finally securing a publisher at fifty-five) has taught me anything, it's that there is no such thing as the *right* age. For marriage. For parenthood. For fulfillment. For finding yourself. We, along with our style, are ever evolving.

As a child, I thought donning my grandmother's mink stole (with the head still intact, which I oddly found glamourous rather than grotesque) while applying Estée perfume on my wrists and crimson rouge on my cheeks made me a lady, a grown-up who knew where she was going in life. In that ensemble, it was clearly out for martinis, but it solidified what I knew to be true—even before my tenth birthday. What I'd wear would shape my identity. Decades later, I cemented this theory as I played dress up for work—coincidentally in the fashion industry, working on fragrance, cosmetics, and ready-to-wear (albeit with no furs, thank you, PETA)—for dates, for an adventurous life in New York City. My character materialized along with my wardrobe.

My forthcoming fashion essay collection trails love, loss, working in fashion, and ultimately finding my authentic self—all told through what I wore—because fashion is so much more than memories and armor; it's the very threads that mold us. From the counterculture rebellion of bell-bottoms and demanding equality in exaggerated power suits to cleansing our palettes from opulence with '90s minimalism and, most recently, sporting athleisure as we (post-pandemic particularly) favor comfort without compromising style, we shape our hearts and souls with our sleeves.

The late *New York Times* style writer Amy Spindler said it best: "[Clothes] can be a mirror of what's inside, or a veneer of camouflage against a world that judges quickly on surfaces, or a map to display your aspirations. You are what you wear, but that turns out to be as complex as you are."

Personally, my white button-downs, pressed and worn habitually, have become more of a cape than an everyday garment. I feel polished and strong, like the fabric itself, even more resilient when the collar stands up. My first luxury purchase, bought on the eve of moving to New York City in the late '90s, remains in rotation today. This uniquely designed Ann Demeulemeester dress was a manifestation of the larger-than-life existence I was striving to lead in my new city; I've prevailed more than I could have even imagined. It doesn't hurt that the dress also taught me the significance of cost-per-wear. As I look back at the clothes that led me to who I am today, I laud them for what they brought me, taught me, and continue to show me about myself.

But just as we've settled into what works—having mastered the art of uniform dressing, established our "three-word method" for shopping ease, and eradicated rules (black and navy are, in fact, brilliant together)—we hit midlife. Or rather, it hits us. Hard.

For me, the shape-shifting power of menopause has been as painful as many of the other symptoms we often encounter. I can disguise a frozen shoulder or joint pain, but bloating and the #MenopauseFifteen have proven far trickier. I would have loved to curl up (in the fetal position, thanks to cramps caused by hormonal fluctuations) and wear a housecoat to wait out the storm, but this tempest can last a decade; we have no option other than to navigate our way through. Fashion, it seems, is not only the best way to express ourselves but is *at every age* the most accessible way to recapture our identity when it shifts during flight.

Ageism may rage on as "the last socially accepted prejudice," but even through my brain fog I recalled what I knew to be true at age ten. Because what we wear can shape who we are—and who we strive to be with each passing decade; while we stop having periods, we never stop having goals—and it can also keep us from those nagging feelings we often experience in midlife. Invisible Woman Syndrome is a genuine phenomenon, and even the most powerful go-getters have felt less than seen or underrepresented despite having more wisdom and a greater sense of self.

"You have to dress for yourself before you dress for your age," legendary fashion icon Iris Apfel once said. While she passed away dressed to the nines at age 102, her mantras luckily live on.

Body composition be damned, I say. I have found that by keeping an open mind, accepting trial and error as creative play, and ignoring cultural vernacular like "age appropriate," my fashion fortitude has not slipped. And when I wear what makes me feel great and true to myself, nothing can conceal me. After all, we don't dress to impress. We dress for ourselves. And, as costume designer Edith Head said, "you can have anything you want in life if you dress for it."

Please STFU and Other Notes on Wearing What I Should

RACHEL SOLOMON

Turns out fifty-plus is the time to explore light bondage gear.

But let me backtrack for a sec. Maybe I've gotten ahead of myself.

I've been fortunate enough to survive my relationship with my body. I say this because I've experienced infinite moments surrounded by women suffering with body and eating issues. (Like that time in law school when there were so many diet concerns among a group of five young women that we couldn't agree on where to eat lunch and ended up separating instead.)

I've always thought, *Thank goodness I managed not to have those problems*. But when I think about how I dress this body, now, at fifty-two, I realize I didn't escape completely. Because I was up to something with my body and clothes. Something like using the advantage of my "socially valued" body (thin, hourglass, big boobs) to…hmmm…to what? I'm wrestling with this. Maybe to make up for not feeling pretty, to "get a man," to feel valued, to please my mom!

This manifested itself in a life spent creating, honing, and refining a uniform designed to "flatter my body" and at times even to...display it to its best advantage. To use it as a means to some end.

Which was a creative prison, style wise. I realize it only now.

I went to Dana Hall, a no-uniform, all-girls' school where I once wore a Lanz nightgown tucked into my gray school sweats with a pair of loafers—which, looking back, was so cool, but not exactly sexy. The change started in college and law school. My mom's "show off your beautiful figure" sentiment collided with my boy-crazy fantasies of being seen, swept up, sexed up, and saved forever by THE ONE. In a series of small (not exactly aha, maybe more like "ooooo") moments, I realized that I had this thing, this tool, that drove a magical response.

So, for example, instead of really getting into the fun of Halloween freshman year of college, I had to show my body at the fraternity party. But I never wanted to look like I was TRYING to show my body. (Sexy nurse was not exactly the MO at Penn with its highly valued nursing school.) So I wore a black knit dress with stars pinned all over it, claiming to be "night." The machinations had begun.

And they went on for decades.

In law school, when others focused on their work and wore sweats, I focused on unattainable men and wore a uniform of Ralph Lauren blanket miniskirts, tights, and fuzzy sweaters. I took the bar exam in a crop top because I thought it might help me with the curve if I could distract anyone around me. At a law firm summer party, I was the only one who swam. In a bright red bikini.

In my first (unhappy, safe) marriage, I desperately craved male attention. I convinced myself that the secret thrill it gave me was normal, wasn't cheating, and was just fun. I held a gaze too long. If guys honked their horns at me, I turned around. If they said I had a nice smile, I couldn't help smiling. And I went dancing with my girlfriends in clothes designed only for this effort: low-rise jeans, G-strings, tank tops with shelf bras. This girl, this lost girl, she's a girl I want to hug. First, though, I'd hand her a cardigan.

And as a divorcée (Is that still a word? Or just on Mad Men?), I teetered in only the highest heels (I remember these Cole Haan cone heel boots; with my hard-earned single-mom salary, I managed the urgently needed black and brown pairs), the jeans with stretch, the DVF dresses—because they flatter!

The sum total of all this? I suspended something I love: personal style. All in service of getting this gaze on me and whatever I imagined it would do for my self-worth and my romantic comedy fairy tale.

*****

There's a picture of me on a boat in Maine at about six, and I've memorized every detail. I have the bob I wear now. The widest smile. I'm leaning confidently back against the rail. You can just tell I feel so completely good. I'm wearing a blue Lilly Pulitzer shift dress that was my favorite, with two stripes of eyelet down the front. And Band-Aids on my knees and elbows. I grin so much at this image now because I know I didn't have cuts—I just liked the way this particular dress looked with Band-Aids. I put each one on deliberately after I put on the dress.

That was personal style! I had an original idea! And I was completely unhindered by what anyone might think, dressing only for myself.

*****

At fifty-two, I've been in my second marriage, a "love marriage" (as they say on *Indian Matchmaking*), for almost fourteen years. It seems to be working, but at this age, wisdom has freed me from my old fairy tale thinking. I laugh watching every twenty-something on reality TV say, "We don't believe in divorce."

I survived the blowout loss that is a broken marriage with a child. In its aftermath, I taught myself that I couldn't afford to be a treasured, fragile, delicate-armed, play-once-in-five-days pitcher; instead, I learned to be a utility player, scrapping and running and gutting it out. Ready to get in the game and make an impact on a moment's notice.

In non-baseball terms: I wised up. And I'm grateful.

All those things that used to get attention I just completely stopped craving. And perfect timing, since this is a decade in which so many of my friends lament "invisibility."

But I don't feel invisible. We made a huge move from cold, judgy Boston to warm, crazy, island-time Miami. And that's made me feel more visible than ever. I interact with so many people in a day, learning Spanish words with our valet guys, waving hi to the security woman in Miu Miu with her daily hairstyle change, greeting Paola, who knows my morning order (Americano, green smoothie, side of eggs) and gives me the "neighbor discount." And I have a new group of girlfriends whom I adore.

I no longer court male attention. I'm free of it. The other day on my walk, a young guy said to me (I was in a Squeeze T-shirt, denim midi, and sparkly shoes), "Mmm, you're looking good, baby," and I truly belly laughed and said, "Like your mom!" My son is twenty! When an old (also married) friend on Facebook made some comment to me about my looking "sexy," I blocked him.

Invisible, or confident, or satisfied, or whatever it is—this is freedom. I mean, as I write this, I'm in a restaurant eating chicken shawarma and chair dancing to "The Tide is High," and I could just scream *I AM SO F***KING HAPPY RIGHT NOW*. Freedom.

And then there's what I'm wearing.

Freed from whatever the body display thing was, I have found my way back to that Band-Aid boat girl. There's been this thread of interest in style my whole life, and I've dipped my pinkie in like I was illicitly tasting more and more cookie batter: a summer job at Ralph Lauren, a story in *InStyle*, writing copy at Rue La La, creative director at M.Gemi, the Italian shoe brand. But my own style? I didn't know what it was under the layers of "for him" stuff.

I'm joyfully rediscovering it. With the help of Instagram as my mirror, support system, and inspiration—thank you, @TrinnyWoodall—and freed from the need to show my figure to its best advantage or whatever, I'm exploring what makes me feel the most like me. It's what personal style, at its best, can be: a joyful way to use the outside to reflect what you feel inside.

In my forties, I started working with a stylist at Saks. I came in armed with all my old rules: I don't wear pencil skirts because of my thighs; I won't wear flats because of my legs. I don't wear ivory or ecru because of my face. I don't wear shorts because of my age. She broke me with one garment: a completely shapeless, short, rectangular ecru Fendi dress that looked like a bathmat on one side and a piece of felt on the other. It made me actually start dancing in the dressing room. And far from caring to "show off his woman," my husband surprised me by deeming it his favorite. "That's cool!" he said. I didn't and don't need his approval—that's the whole point—but honestly it felt so nice to be supported in this way, to be valued for looking cool, not hot. To be appreciated on my own terms in such an important relationship.

The older I get, the closer I get to re-finding that little girl leaning against the boat. I do all kinds of crazy shit in service of my style (emphasis on the *my*), and while I wouldn't say I don't care what anyone thinks, I care very selectively. I share outfits daily on Instagram and love the support, community, and discoveries. But I don't at all care about the "hiding your body" kinds of comments. And I was thrilled when someone called an outfit I put together "modest dressing." In most ways, my dressing really is. I like my body just fine (we all have those fifty whatever cliché complaints), and I work on it. But I don't care to show it off. I am a million times more interested in the cool slouch I get from oversized pants than I am in anyone's knowing whether I'm big or small under there.

And actually, I've noticed that where others want to get into a smaller size, I am much more likely to want bigger. Maybe it's a boomerang reaction. Right now I'm looking for khaki cotton pants and when my stylist friend shows me a pair, I'm like *BIGGER, BIGGER!* To make her understand I said, "One of my cats should be able to sleep inside each leg."

And now back to bondage.

Oh, the irony. It takes freedom to get me to bondage.

Within this finally arrived upon fifty-plus freedom, I haven't remotely considered age in the mix of how I dress. I often dress "modestly" because I just find it cooler. I gravitate toward slouchy and layering. I always have, save for the sexy years, and can remember early days in my dad's old Columbia sweatshirt, the sleeves thinning and fraying in my mouth, and later, the layered polos with the popped collars.

It's funny; in my younger years, anything approaching a bustier or a—gasp!—harness would make me feel desperate and "out there." Not that I didn't try, but when I wore these things I felt naked and unsure and wanting. But now, at this age, my confidence is different and so are the implications. When I play with these items, my age makes it feel fun and subversive, not all-caps SEXY. And I use them as interesting, ironic, and just visually cool elements. I employ little winks—like a Margiela white shirt with a black harness detail in the back made with ribbon. And bigger statements—a white harness over a pinstripe shirt dress, a black silk Khaite harness belt over a white muscle shirt, a zip-front Tibi leather bustier over a white shirt or under a transparent tee. I love anything transparent. Who cares? The other day I wore a bathing suit with a sheer Tibi lantern skirt over it and a white button up on top for a spa day. But when I went to change and go home, I realized I didn't have a bodysuit to go under. So I let the shirt hang out. Sure, if you looked the wrong way for too long you'd see my ass in a thong. And life goes on. No one seemed to notice—and I felt grateful, not invisible.

I love playing around with all of these items. Transparent, leather, bondage-y. I love masculine elements: neckties, suspenders, garter-style socks, boxers peeking out of the top of my skirts. I shop in the men's section too. And I love playing with things that just aren't "pretty," like weird color combinations (red and green, red and brown, purple and yellow) and dark socks inside white sandals. One of my rules in dressing for myself is "if it's not wrong it's not right." I know an outfit, to feel like me, has to have some "off" thing. (I'm writing this in a bustier dress with a muscle tee under it and a pair of distressed tennis sneakers.)

And then there's my biggest—no pun intended—fifty-plus move of all. One of the first things I did in Miami was get a breast reduction. I always imagined if I had plastic surgery, I'd be getting lipo on my thighs. But instead, at fifty-two I was sick of my boobs arriving first to meetings and even more sick of constantly needing to dress around them. They were dictating way too much of my life, especially my style life. So that former "weapon in my arsenal," the very hour in my hourglass? Sayonara, sweeties! It's been real and it's been fun, but you know what? It hasn't been real fun. The real fun starts now when I'm braless at will.

And, oh, when I see women in Miami coffee shops with their beautiful bodies out, their tawny limbs, their boobs rising up like statement chokers, their matching bra and shorts sets, when I watch men's heads swivel after them (this is the invisible piece, maybe, that they swivel in front of me), I smile. I don't think, *Oh, I wish that were me*—I think, *Oh, I want to hug you.* I want to tell them, *Hang in there and weather storms and learn things, and before you know it, you'll be buying yourself the slouchy cardigan of your dreams.*

CHAPTER 11

Notes on Invisibility

Can You See Me Now?

The secret of change is to focus all of your energy not on fighting the old but on building the new.
—*Socrates*

The Not-So-Invisible Woman

DINA ALVAREZ

A funny thing happened to me on my way to midlife—I ceased being invisible. After years of fading into the background and shrinking myself to take up as little space as possible, the wallflower in me finally perked up. A new world unfolded at a time I never expected, in a way I never dreamed.

I've asked myself how something like this happens, how you can spend an entire life feeling invisible and then wake up one day and know things have shifted. The only explanation I can gather is that I'm part of a secret society, a group within the female species tasked with living their lives in reverse. That's how I rationalize it on the outside, but inside, there's always a different story.

I've worn an invisibility cloak as part of my daily dressing all my life. An introvert born to a generation where children were seen and not heard, I excelled at both. I mastered being an adult masquerading as a child. A daughter of strict Cuban immigrant parents and a latchkey kid growing up in the '70s and '80s, I spent a reasonable amount of time quietly adulting myself as best I could, letting books be my parents and, sometimes, parenting my own parents as they maneuvered a new culture and language while raising three kids. I held various grown-up jobs during childhood, including acting as interpreter at my own parent–teacher conferences, the Social Security office, and once, in a crowded courtroom before a judge. The pay sucked.

As a teenager I dated an extrovert and married him the week before my twenty-second birthday. I lived in a self-made world of quiet shyness that introverts simultaneously struggle to break free from while silently wishing they didn't feel so brutalized by their reticence to live out loud. I hid behind my relationship, work, and eventually, my children and life as a mother. In my corporate day job, I leaned toward skirts of proper lengths, blazers, and kitten heels—this time, I felt like a kid acting as an adult.

Amidst bouts of imposter syndrome, caring too much about what other people thought, and grappling with deeply ingrained childhood beliefs of how women should behave, I lacked the ability to think outside the box. I assumed others knew more, ignored my intuition, and often failed to balance expectations—mine and those around me.

Little did I know that years later, I would make up for lost time. That in midlife, a time we've been programmed to dread, I would feel more visible than ever. I just had to get there. There were a few things to unlearn, (the relentless need to people please), wounds to re-open and stitch back together, (acknowledging that my parents did the best they could), and several conversations that needed to be had, mostly with myself.

Ironically, as my life expanded, a new form of invisibility arrived. I became familiar with sitting in a restaurant and having the server direct the conversation and eye contact toward my husband. Male or female, it didn't matter. The cashier couldn't bother to look up. The deli guy took the young woman's order before mine even though I was there first, and the bartender took his sweet time coming over. It wasn't about *wanting* attention; I rarely garnered it, even in my youthful glory days, which are only apparent to me now in the photo albums I occasionally take down from the top shelf of the closet. Nor did I ever expect it; I knew how to fly under the radar, but I didn't appreciate having anyone else push me into the background. Only I was allowed to make myself invisible.

Except then, everyone became invisible.

The pandemic arrived, and along with it, a personal shutdown that slowly chipped away the old to build the new. I questioned everything and reached a space where self-acceptance and a mental transformation formed an alliance. The physical overhaul arrived by default and crashed the party. I got rid of the boring blunt haircut and grew out my hair because I had no choice. I donated the mom jeans, shoved the corporate skirts and heels to the back of the closet, and began experimenting with new ways of dressing. I moved away from the extreme workwear of corporate life and embraced the flowing, open state of someone drawn to her own ease of character while still holding on to the structure she needed to feel pulled together. The blazers stayed.

I used my time to eat well and exercise. I avoided the news after it saturated me to my very core. Instead, I read books and listened to music that nourished my soul. I slept the dark circles right off my face. I reconnected with myself and loved who I was becoming, and when the world opened up again, I was ready. I became an outgoing introvert. Slowly. The pay wasn't bad.

And then, in what I would never have considered the next logical step, I whimsically posted one photo of myself online. Clad in jeans, a plaid shirt, and an army green jacket, I stepped onto a platform I eschewed forever. Whether it was lockdown boredom, a need for creative expression, or the desire to feel that I was taking up space in the world, I can't say for sure, but after a self-imposed decade-long hiatus from pitching and publishing

DINA ALVAREZ & DINA ARONSON

articles, I began to write again—and in ways that seemed to connect. I started with a few photos and short captions, then, eventually, longer anecdotes and stories. My family stood around confused. "You?" they asked. "The introvert? The private person? The one who hides from the camera at all costs?" It was hard for them. Maybe they needed a minute to reconcile who I was with who I was becoming, but I wasn't deterred. I wasn't going back again. I never wanted to be the version of me that stood at the financial aid office counter after being accepted into an overpriced dream school, and when no one acknowledged me after fifteen minutes—just the right amount of time to doubt myself—turned around and left. I chose another (and thankfully cheaper) college.

Maybe I wouldn't have graduated from that school. Maybe I would have realized I had no interest in going into debt for a degree that might not guarantee me any kind of lucrative career, but I would have at least liked to have been seen that day, to have slammed my hand on the counter and said, "Hello, (insert expletive here)! Someday I'm going to write about your trite asses." Yet that side of me, the one who did nothing, had to live to tell the story but also die—except killing off a piece of yourself is nearly impossible. Instead, I forgave her for the stranglehold she'd kept me in and relegated her to the past where she belonged.

It's hard to believe that a few photos and a foray into microblogging could be a catalyst for change, but that's what feeling visible does to a woman—the stories I shared, drawn from my personal life and the common themes we all inhabit, took hold. Everything from run-ins with famous people to trying to gracefully shut down a dinner party in my home when a conversation leaned into politics and took a turn for the worse.

I was asked if I had plans to write a book, and these people, who I did not know in real life, the ones who left kind comments and spurred me on, led me to places I never imagined. The pay was getting better. In fact, I'd finally gotten a raise.

This newfound visibility pushed me out of my comfort zone and gave me the confidence I was missing all along. I asked questions with ease. I smiled more. My demeanor changed. I stopped apologizing unnecessarily. I approached random strangers and started conversations, a few of which led to new collaborations and connections I'd never anticipated. I was asked out on a date, the deli guy knew my name, and the bartender gave me a head nod—eventually. I developed a presence and voice I'd never known, one that aided in cultivating worthwhile friendships and ignited the courage to launch creative projects, including the very book you hold in your hands. Another part of stepping out of the dark and into the light. All in midlife.

My invisibility cloak hasn't fully retired; I still wear it when the mood strikes. If only I could use it to hide from the torn meniscus that appeared for no apparent reason, or that feeling I get when I leave my eighty-three-year-old mother and, as I lean in to kiss her, wonder if it could be the last time we see each other. But when it comes to aging and feeling invisible, I've had a very different and unforeseen latter life experience. Whereas in my first part of life I felt completely unseen, this decade has made up for it. If I am invisible to others, I honestly don't notice it. I'm too caught up enjoying the road I'm on now more than any other, out loud, creatively, and with no holds barred. The truth is, I don't require the attention of the world; I get all I need from those who matter—the ones who see me and, with their kind words, embrace me, no matter what age I am.

Invisible? Not anymore.

The Crumbling Palazzo

JODY DAY

Having come through a classic early-forties clusterf**k of infertility, divorce, childlessness, and extended singleness, I found myself in my early fifties feeling pretty good about things. Sure, the prospect of meeting a new life partner looked as likely as finding a flattering swimsuit, but all things considered, getting old didn't look *too* bad.

And then I went back to Italy, where my young womanhood had been introduced to its *allure* after the inept fumblings of my English countrymen. After a transformative year as a Roman au pair, I used to joke that the only thing a woman had to do to get male attention in Italy was to "wake up and have a pulse." I took what felt at that time like a worldly knowing back to London with me and, my wardrobe and confidence transformed, took it as my birthright.

Fast-forward: I was fifty-one and spending a two-week holiday by the sea with one of those Roman charmers from my past, along with his wife and children. After a delightfully rambunctious week embedded in family life, I was looking forward to my planned week alone—time to write, to wander, and to wonder about my future. I'd been peacefully celibate for several years by this point, but I vaguely entertained the notion that should the opportunity present itself, I might have a little dalliance with the opposite sex. Perhaps flickering in the projection room of my mind was one of those backlit movies where bereft middle-aged women find romance, even love, in Italy, usually with a crumbling palazzo involved.

One evening, after a productive day writing in cafés, I'd freshened up and headed to a local restaurant. I sat contentedly alone, devouring the menu and the bread basket and, as the place began to fill up, enjoyed the theater of Italian life unfolding around me. Thus it took a while for me to notice that I'd nearly finished my wine, but still nobody had come to take my order. I tried to catch my waiter's eye, both of my hands clasped around my menu, clearly looking ready, while couples who'd come in after me welcomed their food. And then, just as my hunger and annoyance propelled me to my feet to request service, a young woman walked in, a gust of wind misting her hair into a halo, and time stopped as the waiters flowed toward her like a river to the sea. She was probably in her early twenties, not particularly beautiful by Italian standards, and I observed through an almost anthropological lens the biological uproar she evoked. Men sitting with their female partners glanced up too, as the manager, maître d', and waiters hustled for position around her. Seemingly unaware of her impact, she booked her table for two, and once the door had been lovingly closed behind her, the men came out of their trance, and the clockwork restaurant restarted. My waiter saw me standing there, menu in hand, a wry smile on my face. "Ah, signora," he said, with a bashful half smile and a soft shake of his head as he walked me sedately back to my table, pulling out my chair and taking my order.

Signora!

I ate my delicious food without pleasure that evening, my joy squashed by the realization that I'd crossed the Rubicon of f**kabilty and that, like the consuls that Caesar had routed,

Rome would no longer open its gates to me. I was *Signora* now, an object of respect, not desire. I was defeated.

Over the next few days, unable to sit comfortably in my skin and propelled to endless walking and rumination by the orchestra of unbidden sighs that arose from me, I recognized that I was grieving. Something had irrevocably gone from my life—my youth—and with it my social currency with the opposite sex. Much as I'd been enjoying the serenity of sitting out the dance of courtship, it made all the difference when I'd thought it was a *choice*; discovering that my dance card had expired shook me to the core. Like all privilege, I had taken my youth and attractiveness for granted and had been quite dismissive of how it had opened doors for me in the world of men, the world as we know it. Now I couldn't even get served in an Italian restaurant.

Back in London, I explored my new awareness with friends, only to be met with reassurances about my looks, which entirely missed the point. I wasn't looking for an ego boost; I was grappling for a language to express this loss of something ineffable that I'd taken for granted all my adult life. But instead, I was told to take Helen Mirren as an example of foxiness in older women, the fact that I've never aspired to foxiness seemingly irrelevant.

Ironically, later that year, I did meet a new partner, an Englishman my age, and we've been together ever since. Having both come through long-term breakups years before, we were each only willing to trade our now-treasured peace of mind for a partnership of equals. Over the last eight years, we've cared for and lived through the deaths of both our mothers, two country relocations, a pandemic, and building what we hope will be our "forever home." Now in our sixties, we're dealing with health issues that require careful management and, as the older generation departs, are stepping into their shoes. We're doing our best to stay awake to the known-unknowns of aging without children, set against a backdrop of civilizational uncertainty. Nothing can be taken for granted anymore.

So far, so smug.

Having done a good deal of conscious work facing up to aging and death as part of my infertility and childlessness, I felt well prepared for the road ahead. But it turned out that I'd been looking forward to aging *theoretically*, anticipating it as a time of deeper transformation, a chance to shed the drama of my earlier years and see what this new perspective might bring. I was lofty, philosophical, spiritual. It seems I'd blanked out the bone-chilling memories of previous transformations, which, as opposed to the butterfly motif so beloved of Instagram Lite quotes, were more those of a bewildered and outraged caterpillar, metamorphosing against its will inside a jacket of hardened saliva, its body turning to mush, with absolutely no idea what was going on. In my hubris, I'd forgotten all about my body, the very vehicle this theoretical transformation would take place through, until one day, catching sight of myself supine in a new Pilates class and an unknown mirror, I didn't recognize myself.

How could this be me?

And worse, I was ashamed of her. I despised her, this matronly lump lying on the slab of the Pilates machine, her midsection hefty even while horizontal. I wanted to disown her, this lazy, greedy, misshapen old woman, and, in that hatred, I heard the harpies that had driven my mother's lifelong dietary hypervigilance circle around me, cackling, *Gotcha!* Getting home later that day, I planned to starve myself into nonexistence, to punish the flesh that offended me as if it were an obscene growth to be excised and disposed of, rather than the perfectly normal outcome of hormones, illness, gravity, and aging. I caught myself as I boiled with self-hatred and internalized ageism, remembering how I'd punished my body for my infertility and how, through the practice of self-compassion and gratitude, I'd befriended her again. I was going to have to do so all over again. And again. I sensed that this was just the beginning.

I used to fantasize that if I'd had the joy of children and grandchildren, maybe I wouldn't objectify my body in the same way. But then I remembered my mother grabbing a roll of my fleshy midsection when I'd visited her once in her nursing home. "What's this?!" she'd said with gleeful spite, my body forever an extension of hers. "It's my menopausal middle," I responded calmly, years of not rising to the bait in action, and she huffed her emaciated, dementia-ravaged body back onto the pillows and drifted elsewhere. Even as her awareness of her own body broke down, she could still find fault with mine.

I dreamt that a younger, firmer, slimmer version of my body stepped out of my skin, shedding it like a coat. I felt light and free and strong. I looked back at my old body lying discarded on the ground like a pelt, and walked away.

During my ninety-three-year-old mother-in-law's dying days, I remember massaging moisturizer into her scaly shins, powdering under her hanging breasts to prevent sores, and spritzing her with her favorite perfume. Her body was a crumbling palazzo, entirely beyond repair but filled with memories of dancing, parties, love, and laughter.

She left it in ruins.

When I was a young girl, I remember hanging myself upside-down from trees and twisting myself into pretzels of joy as I copied the moves of Russian Olympic gymnast Olga Korbut from the TV. That version of Jody didn't know she had a body; she *was* a body. Somehow, I need to find my way back to her.

I turn to pick that unwanted dream pelt off the floor and shrug it back on. I will not abandon her again.

CHAPTER 12

The Last Place I Ever Thought I'd Be

*Life offers us tickets to places which we
have not knowingly asked for.*
—Maya Angelou

The Last Place I Ever Thought I'd Be

NATALIE Y. WESTER

The moment you step foot in the Oval Office of the White House everything becomes a surreal blur. I was warned beforehand by previous teacher honorees to be sure to look around and take in every detail of this storied office, "because you'll never again in life have the chance to see it." This was the last place I ever thought I'd be.

We had to wait in line for our turn with the president of the United States. Handlers lined us up outside in the smoldering heat and humidity, according to, of all things, our height. I was very last, thanks to being six-foot-two in my heels, and by the time it was finally my turn, my freshly done hair had wilted, and my nerves had erased everything I'd planned to say to the president of our country. All I managed to spit out initially was, "Hello, Mr. President! I guess I'm the tallest teacher in the land!" Oh. My. God. I eventually got it together enough to hand him a book of advice my third-grade students had written for him, and he was gracious enough to suggest taking two photos together—one with the book and one "official" shot. Then I was escorted back outside to take my place standing on the back row of risers in the hot sun of the Rose Garden, where I tried not to pass out during a long ceremony of speeches and musical performances. I couldn't believe it. This was the last place I ever thought I'd be.

But it wasn't the first time I'd ended up in the last place I ever thought I'd be. Nearly twenty-five years before I walked into the Oval Office, I lay on a hospital ICU bed with my wrists restrained. At twenty-seven, this was the last place I ever thought I'd be. I'd regained consciousness two days after very nearly succeeding at committing suicide. I was supposed to be dead, and this was not where I wanted to be.

When you see suicidal people portrayed in the movies, they are often despondent and tearful. But my decision and subsequent planning to end my life at twenty-seven was my happiest, most contented period back then. There was a powerful sense of freedom and control as I researched the Hemlock Society, ordered its suicide how-to manual, began stockpiling necessary supplies, and worked with a lawyer to write my will. I am nothing if not organized, and planning my suicide—what was supposed to be my first and last "solo trip"—was no different. I had a to-do list and timetable. Other than these secret preparations, there were no outward indications of my suicidal state, no warning signs anyone could pick up from my demeanor.

I followed all the tips in the manual, except for pulling a plastic bag over my head and tying it shut around my neck immediately after taking the pills. That sounded claustrophobic and scary. On a Saturday afternoon, I sat in the kitchen of my apartment and ate a light snack of plain soda crackers, to put something in my stomach to guard against vomiting up the pills. I crushed a bottle of Percocet tablets in a tall glass, then emptied Fioricet capsules into the glass as well. I poured in Jack Daniel's, stirred the mixture, then topped it off with ginger ale. I drank the entire glass of fizzy, gritty liquid with white-laced foam on top, taking breaks between gulps to nibble crackers as suggested. When I'd swallowed all the liquid, I poured a little more ginger ale into the glass, swished it around to get all the white pill residue from the sides, and then swallowed that down. I didn't cry. I wasn't afraid. The Jack Daniel's made me woozy right away. It was years later before I could drink or even smell whiskey or ginger ale without gagging.

I went to my bedroom, double-checked that my will and note were on the nightstand, and lay down on my bed, willing myself not to vomit as my stomach began lurching, trying to save the life I was determined to end. I should be dead now. But the phone next to my bed rang (no cell phones back then) as I was falling asleep for the last time. I say I answered the phone because I was nearly unconscious and didn't know what I was doing. Some say I didn't really want to die. Either way, answering that phone saved my life. I lifted the receiver but wasn't responsive, and my friend called 911.

Rescuers broke in and had to perform a tracheotomy there on my bed. The bloody sheets were a shock when I returned to the apartment after being released from the hospital, a reminder of violence committed undercover. This was the last place I ever thought I'd be.

That twenty-seven-year-old is a stranger now. Like walking into the Oval Office, that old life seems surreal. Now I think about all the times since then that I've uttered, "This was the last place I ever thought I'd be." When, at thirty, I became the first Black vice president of the oldest independent PR firm in the country. When I became a business owner at thirty-one. When I became a mother at thirty-four. When I went back to graduate school for another master's degree at forty-five, then started a second career as a teacher. When I met the president five years later. When I retired as a single, fifty-nine-year-old woman. When I traveled around the world solo for seventy days for my sixtieth birthday. And when I started an internship at a whiskey distillery of all places at sixty-one. This was the last place I ever thought I'd be. But I had underestimated the power of tomorrow. Tomorrows keep taking me to the places I never thought I'd be. And yet here I am. Again and again.

A version of this essay first appeared in Women On Writing, *where it placed in the publication's 2022 Q2 Creative Nonfiction Essay Contest.*

Infinitely You

your value
your strengths
and talents
are infinite
and evolving

make up your mind
not to hide
from your fears
or insecurities
but give yourself
enough love
to tolerate when they arise

your vulnerability
is where change begins

allow the joy of spontaneity
to lead you
to places in this world
where you will be supported
loved and safe

so your truest self
can thrive
helping others
to do the same

—*Laureen Benevenia*

Afterword

The very existence of this book is proof that it is never too late and that you are never too old to shift gears or try something new. It is also a testament to the fact that midlife, even with all its transitions, upheavals, and attendant challenges, can be a fertile (pun intended) time for self-discovery, growth, and creativity, a time to bloom in new and perhaps unexpected ways.

It's striking that a book of essays along a particular theme could have an underlying and unexpected thread that we never anticipated—one we didn't see until the very end as we compiled the manuscript for a final review.

As the dream to put this anthology together unfolded, the pandemic was at the end of its first year. Under lockdown, disconnected and processing a once-in-a-lifetime event left us all unmoored. Yet at the same time, as the world shut down, it offered a chance to step back in a way that we would have never done before. For some it was a respite—an opportunity to hunker down and work on the other sides of ourselves that are often left to the world of "somedays" we think will come. For others, grief and loss solidified how everything can change in an instant.

The willingness to say *yes* seemed to emerge as another theme as we collected these stories. Whether it was saying yes to trying something new, yes to giving themselves permission to change their minds, yes to letting go of limiting thoughts or other things that did not serve, or yes to ultimately accepting and flowing with change, in some way each of these essays illustrate the expansive power of being open to change and to new possibilities. Saying yes was the catalyst for our new midlife friendship and collaboration, and in return the universe sent us a host of women eager to say yes to us.

The idea to tell our midlife stories springs from rich tradition—throughout history women have been storytellers, shaping our worlds to keep our ancestral connections alive. As much as we've progressed, the practice of storytelling remains an art, an integral part of the way we communicate and connect with one another. For all our differences, the stories we tell also highlight how, in many ways, we share so much as fellow travelers.

Let's keep telling our stories, and encourage others to bravely tell theirs, so that women everywhere will be inspired to change the way they think about age.

Acknowledgments

First, thank you dear readers for spending some of your precious time here with us; we see you, and we hope that these stories spoke to you and made you feel like part of a big, beautiful midlife sisterhood, one that is rewriting the rules and aging boldly, without apology.

Without our amazing contributors, you would not be holding this book in your hands. We are forever grateful to them for trusting us with their stories and revelations. Thank you all for saying yes, and thank you for sharing our vision to help midlife women everywhere feel seen, heard, and understood, and more broadly, to shift the cultural conversation around women and age. We've been blown away by the generosity of spirit of this group, and we hope you will visit the contributors page to learn more about these brilliant women, many of whom serve midlife women in some important way. Special thanks to Sari Botton, who encouraged us early on and shared her expertise; to Katie Fogarty, who made so many incredible introductions; to Laura Geller, who pushed us to think bigger; and to Jessica Fein, who connected us to the woman who would become our agent.

Books of essays can be hard to sell, let alone essays about midlife women. Thank you to our agent, Michele Martin, who didn't let that stop her from taking us on, and whose patience, guidance, and wisdom helped to get us over the finish line.

Special thanks goes to Debra Englander, who saw the value in telling these stories and believed in this project as much as we did; Caitlin Burdette who kept us organized and on track, and Lucy VanBerkum for her smart editorial guidance. A big thanks also goes to Gretchen Young and Regalo Press for giving two first-time authors the opportunity to bring a book to life.

To all of our cheerleaders and unofficial advisers, thank you. Every time we mentioned this project to the people in our orbit (or anyone outside of it who would listen), we were met with resounding enthusiasm and genuine interest, which motivated us and kept our momentum going and our spirits high. So to old friends, new friends, people on the subway, people in grocery lines, and so on, thank you!

To our families, and in particular, to our husbands, Roger and Eric, who supported this project unconditionally and who both graciously and without complaint sat through countless marathon Zoom calls, some lasting ten-plus hours(!), while we fully ignored them and everything else going on around us and worked on this book. We love you both and promise to give you a little break before we start the next one!

We had no idea what to expect when we started down this road; we are living, breathing examples of the idea that it is never too late, and that you don't need to have all the answers before starting something new. In fact, we had very few answers, but we did have a strong desire to connect with other midlife women and show, through the power of storytelling, that even when we feel alone on this transitional road, we are in good company.

Thank you to the universe of midlife women out there who inspired us to tell these stories.

Contributors

Marian Adams was born in 1964 and is one of six children. She grew up in a large Irish family on Long Island, never far from any of her fifty-six first cousins. She received a master of fine arts from Saint Michael's College in 1986 and worked in public relations post-college in New York City. She loves books, movies, cooking, and the ocean. Marian married her childhood sweetheart, a United States Marine, in 1989. They settled on Long Island with their three children after several years on the West Coast. Marian is honored and grateful to share her story in the hope that it will empower women to advocate for themselves when it comes to their health. Her wish is that all women will be better equipped than she was to navigate the many challenging medical issues they may face in midlife.

Wendi Aarons is an award-winning humor writer and author of *I'm Wearing Tunics Now*; the middle-grade book *Ginger Mancino, Kid Comedian*; and *Socks*. Her satire frequently appears in *The New Yorker* and *McSweeney's*, and she is also a regular contributor to *Texas Monthly* and various other outlets. Her humor pieces have been performed by award-winning actresses, including Uzo Aduba, Sharon Horgan, and *Glow*'s Alison Brie. Wendi both speaks on and teaches humor writing to both children and adults, and lives in Austin.

Laura Belgray, author of national bestseller *Tough Titties: On Living Your Best Life When You're the F-ing Worst*, is also the founder of Talking Shrimp and co-creator of The Copy Cure with Marie Forleo. She has been featured in *Elle*, *Fast Company*, *Money Magazine*, *Forbes*, *Vox*, and *Business Insider*, and has written for Bravo, Fandango, FX, NBC, HBO, USA, Nick at Nite, Nickelodeon, TV Land, VH1, and more. Laura lives with her husband in New York and, except for college, has never lived anywhere else. Not coincidentally, she doesn't drive.

Laureen Benevenia graduated from New York University with a Journalism degree, and went on to a career in advertising and marketing. Retired, she now enjoys new creative pursuits, and shares her writing and poetry about the beauty of aging across several platforms, including her popular Instagram account, @GlowUpSilver, where she also documents her journey to embrace her grey hair. Laureen is passionate about working to shift the aging narrative, and showing women by example that midlife is a time of transformation, new beginnings, and great possibility. She had her first essay published in Alpha Magazine at age fifty four, and signed with Stetts Management as a model, representing midlife women in national campaigns for companies like Lancome, Warners, Malia Mills, Moderna, and Bank of America. She also works as user-generated content creator and has partnered with brands like Clarins, Laura Mercier, Rōz, and Mother Science. She also volunteers her time with the national online platform Crisis Text Line. Laureen resides in New Jersey with her husband and their three-year-old goldendoodle who joined the family when their youngest moved out.

Sari Botton is the author of a memoir in essays, *And You May Find Yourself…Confessions of a Late-Blooming Gen-X Weirdo*, which was chosen by *Poets & Writers* magazine for the 2022 edition of its annual 5 Over 50 feature. An essay from it received notable mention in *The Best American Essays 2023*, edited by Vivian Gornick. For five years, she was the essays editor at *Longreads*. She edited the bestselling anthologies *Goodbye to All That: Writers on Loving and Leaving New York* and *Never Can Say Goodbye: Writers on Their Unshakable Love for New York*. She publishes *Oldster Magazine*, *Memoir Land*, and the Substack *Adventures in Journalism*. She was the writer in residence in the creative writing department at SUNY New Paltz for spring 2023.

Jody Day is the English/Irish founder of Gateway Women, the global support and advocacy network for childless women, and is often described as the founder of the "childless movement." An author, two-time TEDx speaker, thought leader, and psychotherapist, she's known for her bestselling *Living the Life Unexpected: How to Find Hope, Meaning and a Fulfilling Future Without Children* (PanMac, 2016/2020) and increasingly for her popular Substack, *Gateway Elderwomen*, which explores the adventure of elderhood without motherhood. Jody's been a World Childless Week Ambassador since its inception in 2017 and was chosen as one of the BBC's 100 Women in 2013 and as a UK Digital Woman of the Year in 2021. She was also a founding and former board member at the UK charity Aging Without Children and is a former fellow in social innovation at Cambridge Judge Business School. She recently trained as a Work That Reconnects facilitator to weave into her *Gateway Elderwomen* project focused on disrupting ageism, facilitating intergenerational connections, and creating a pilot study of how to build an "Alterkin" (alternative kinship network) mutual-aid community of care for those aging without children. She lives in rural Ireland and hopes to finish her first novel soon. Jody can be found at Gateway-Women.com.

Gabriella Espinosa is a women's health and sexual wellness coach and the host of *Pleasure in the Pause*, a podcast dedicated to empowering midlife women to embrace their pleasure, power, and purpose through perimenopause, menopause, and beyond. Drawing from fifteen years of experience, Gabriella's work integrates embodiment practices, Eastern wisdom traditions, female sexuality, and menopausal health. She has guided count-less women to reconnect with and trust their bodies through one-on-one coaching, group programs, online courses, and international retreats. Gabriella views menopause as a power-ful opportunity for self-discovery and transformation, helping women emerge wiser, stronger, sexier, and more empowered. Her approach invites women to embark on a journey of deep self-exploration and trust. Gabriella lives in Austin, Texas, with her husband and is the proud mother of three young adults. Learn more at PleasureInThePause.com.

Maryjane Fahey is on her fifth reinvention as founder of Glorious Broads, the epicenter of confident, unconventional Broads over 50. She cut her teeth in print, art directing, rebrand-ing, and launching magazines from *Fast Company* and *Women's Health* to *The Boston Globe*, then rode the internet tsunami as launching creative and content editor of AARP's Disrupt Aging, challenging old concepts and assumptions the world has about aging. She's written for *Bustle*, *The Zoe Report*, *HuffPost*, *Next*, and *NPR* and has been featured in ABC News and *Cosmo*'s breakthrough special *Sex After 60* wearing next to nothing and saying next to everything. Maryjane co-authored a book called *DUMPED*, a hilarious guide to getting over a breakup in record time. Living in New York City, she continues her role renewing, reinventing, and speaking out about what it means to stay relevant, passionate, and a viable, celebrated woman—at any age. Maryjane is presently developing a steamy TV series for Glorious Broads.

Jessica Fein is the author of *Breath Taking: A Memoir of Family, Dreams, and Broken Genes* and host of the *I Don't Know How You Do It* podcast, which features people whose lives seem unimaginable from the outside. Her writing has appeared in *The New York Times, Newsweek, Psychology Today, The Boston Globe, HuffPost, Scary Mommy, Kveller,* and more. Jessica's work encompasses hope and humor, grit and grace—the tools that make up her personal survival kit. To learn more, visit JessicaFeinStories.com.

Julie Flakstad is a speaker, writer, and founder of *The Midlife Truth Project*, a research-based platform and podcast aimed at unraveling the myriad of transitions that women face as they settle into their forties and fifties. Having created and produced over 350 events, workshops, and programs on women's issues, Julie is passionate about bringing voices together around complex and vulnerable topics. She's regularly featured in podcasts about midlife transition and in various publications, including Maria Shriver's *Sunday Paper, Forbes,* and Katie Couric Media. Follow her @JulieFlakstad and learn more at JulieFlakstad.com.

Katie Fogarty is a podcaster, pro-age advocate, and host of the top-ranked podcast *A Certain Age*, a show that celebrates women forty, fifty, and sixty-plus who are aging out loud. She also hosts the literary podcast *The Midlife Book Club*. A former journalist and PR executive, Katie also runs a career coaching company and sits on the boards of Let's Talk Menopause and Flow Space and tries to talk her husband and three adult-ish kids into sweating it out at hot yoga with her. Follow Katie on Instagram @ACertainAgePod and @TheMidlifeBookClub.

Laura Geller began a love affair with beauty at an early age, a passion that led her to become a successful makeup artist, working under the bright lights of Broadway and behind the scenes with celebrities and socialites. It was Laura's devotion to making makeup work for real women that led her to create her own beauty brand, believing that beauty is for everyone and should be uncomplicated, inclusive, and fun. Since her very first appearance on QVC in 1997 and throughout the twenty successful years her Upper East Side makeup studio was open, Laura has used tips and tricks to translate professional application into techniques that work for all women, every day. In 2012, *Crain's New York Business* recognized Laura as one of its Top Entrepreneurs of the Year. Laura is also a recipient of the 2014 Cosmetic Executive Women Achiever Award. Laura was honored at the CEW Foundation's Beauty of Giving event in 2016 for her work. Since 2021, the brand has partnered with actress and activist Fran Drescher to support her Cancer Schmancer initiative that works toward cancer prevention and early detection. Laura herself is a breast cancer survivor and serves on the board of Cancer + Careers, an organization working to support cancer patients and survivors in the workplace, as well as the Dubin Breast Center of the Tisch Cancer Institute at Mount Sinai Hospital in New York City. In 2023, Laura was named to *Forbes* 50 Over 50. Born and raised in New York, Laura is a single mother to her son Daniel. Follow Laura on Instagram @LauraGellerBeauty and @LauraJGeller.

Mary Claire Haver, MD, FACOG, CMP, is a board-certified obstetrician and gynecologist who graduated from Louisiana State University Medical Center and completed her residency at the University of Texas Medical Branch (UTMB). She is also a certified culinary medicine specialist and a Menopause Society certified menopause practitioner. In 2021, she established Mary Claire Wellness, a clinic dedicated to providing comprehensive care for menopausal patients. In 2023, she published her first book, *The Galveston Diet*, and launched ThePauseLife.com as a trusted resource for menopausal women worldwide. With over four million followers on social media, Dr. Haver is recognized as a thought leader and author who provides valuable advice for women going through different stages of menopause. She aims to "demystify menopause" and promote self-advocacy for women's health. This led her to publish her second book, *The New Menopause*, which became a No. 1 *New York Times* bestseller.

Susan Heinrich is a Canadian writer based in Denver, Colorado. She began her career as a journalist at Canada's *National Post* before transitioning to freelance writing while raising her two sons. After relocating from Toronto to Denver, Susan studied novel writing and literary craft at the renowned Lighthouse Writers Workshop, where she participated in workshops with authors such as Andre Dubus III and Kazuo Ishiguro. In 2020, she founded *Midlife Globetrotter*, a website and platform to help women forty-plus follow their travel dreams to new places. Susan is passionate about reframing midlife as an opportunity and explores themes of reinvention and self-discovery in her work. Susan is a member of the North American Travel Journalists Association. She has two young-adult sons and lives with her husband, Sean, and a quirky rescue dog, Archie. She is currently completing her debut novel.

Rachel Hughes is a graduate of Vassar College and a former dancer with the Alvin Ailey American Dance Theater. She holds an MSEd from Bank Street College in New York City, specializing in early childhood and museum education. Later, she became a licensed nutritional counselor, dedicating over a decade to working with chronic pain patients at the New England Center for Chronic Pain in Greenwich, Connecticut. She has authored several publications on a range of health conditions, including IBS, tinnitus, and fibromyalgia. When Rachel experienced disruptive perimenopausal symptoms, she embarked on a journey to find clarity and actionable information. In 2020, she joined the Perry platform, where she launched and hosted *Perry Talks*, a series of live interviews with physicians, experts, and thought leaders on all things related to perimenopause and menopause. Her leadership helped the Perry community grow into the No. 1 menopause community app, fostering a space for women to share experiences and find support. Currently, Rachel is the Community Manager at Alloy Women's Health, where she is committed to bridging the gap between women facing peri/ menopause symptoms and the science-based solutions that can improve their lives. She leads support groups and hosts webinars and IG conversations providing data-driven, expert-led discussions on hormonal health. Through her work, Rachel creates inclusive spaces where women can connect, share their stories, and receive evidence-based support from medical professionals.

Michelle Jacobs is the Co-Founder and COO of Womaness, a brand that is changing the conversation around aging, midlife, and menopause through innovative products in skincare, supplements, and sexual wellness. Womaness provides clinically and doctor-tested products and trusted advice on symptoms from hot flashes to sleep issues to fine lines, and support from an inspired community of women. Prior to Womaness, Michelle spent twenty years in corporate marketing and brand building positions at Pfizer, Time, Inc., and HSN. Michelle earned her BA from Colgate University and MBA from NYU Stern. She lives in Larchmont, New York, with her family.

Susan Kanoff is a former social worker and wardrobe stylist, as well as the founder of Uncommon Threads, a nonprofit that empowers low-income women through clothing and personal styling. Founded in 2016, Susan started the organization to combine her passion for fashion with her commitment to helping women build self-esteem and confidence. Also known as *The Midlife Fashionista*, Susan's blog and social media accounts offer fashion, beauty, and wellness tips for women over forty. She has been featured in *Woman's World* magazine and *The Boston Globe*, and on Boston television stations WGBH, NECN, and WCVB. Susan lives with chronic lymphocytic leukemia (CLL), and she co-founded CLL Women Strong, the first national support group for women living with CLL, and Kicking Cancer in Heels, an online platform to bring resources and hope to women impacted by cancer. She has won many awards for her work supporting women and families, including a Massachusetts state citation for excellence, NAHRO awards for program innovation, and the YWCA Tribute to Women Award, and she was named a 2022 *Northshore Magazine* Mover & Shaker.

Sarah Milken is the creator and host of the podcast *The Flexible Neurotic*, where she and her female listeners explore reinventing themselves in the second half of life together. Sarah is inspiring midlife women to focus on themselves and to dig deep (her show's symbol is a golden shit shovel) to uncover new possibilities for their lives. Sarah has amassed thousands of Instagram followers and has created a dedicated and engaged community with her podcast, which ranks in the top 1 percent. Sarah graduated with honors from the University of Pennsylvania with a BA in communications and went on to receive her PhD in educational psychology at the University of Southern California, after which she taught in the graduate school of education at USC. She has served on several philanthropic boards as well as the board of a Los Angeles private school. After taking time off to raise her two children (now teens), she realized she needed to recreate herself and capitalize on all of her strengths, hence *The Flexible Neurotic* podcast was born. Sarah and her husband, Jeremy, live in Pacific Palisades, California. They are currently half-empty nesters, with one twelfth-grade daughter at home and their son currently attending the University of Pennsylvania.

Christine Morrison is a freelance journalist known for bringing a fresh lens to the topic of aging. Her writing has appeared in print and online vehicles such as *The Washington Post, The Boston Globe, The Quality Edit,* and *Margot Magazine,* among others, and in advertising campaigns for Alastin Skincare, French Connection, Juicy Couture, and more. Prior to focusing on writing full-time, Morrison held leadership positions in the fashion and beauty industries, including serving as global vice president of beauty and apparel marketing for Calvin Klein. A sought-after brand-builder, she also launched innovative products and advertising campaigns for clients such as Biore, Curel, John Frieda, and Olay while at Leo Burnett, Saatchi & Saatchi, and JWT. She is currently a member of THE BOARD, a collective of fractional talent experts. Her forthcoming book, *Clothes Minded: Fashionable Essays About Finding Yourself*—in which she reflects on the meaning behind, and the humor in, the relationship between her sartorial self and formation of identity—is slated to publish Spring 2026.

Zibby Owens is the author of *Blank: A Novel*; *Bookends: A Memoir of Love, Loss, and Literature*, and children's book *Princess Charming*, and the editor of three anthologies: *On Being Jewish Now*, *Moms Don't Have Time to Have Kids*, and *Moms Don't Have Time To: A Quarantine Anthology*. Her next novel, *Overheard*, is forthcoming. A frequent contributor to Good Morning America and Katie Couric Media, she has contributed to *Vogue*, Oprah Daily, *The Washington Post*, and other outlets, and has appeared on CNN, CBS This Morning, and many others. *Vulture* called her "NYC's Most Powerful Book-fluencer." Zibby is also the CEO and Founder of Zibby Media, dubbed "the Zibby-verse" by *The Los Angeles Times*, which includes the award-winning daily podcast *Totally Booked with Zibby* (formerly known as *Moms Don't Have Time to Read Books)*; the boutique publishing house Zibby Books; Zibby's Bookshop, an independent bookstore in Santa Monica, California; Zibby's Book Club; and Zibby Retreats and events for book lovers. A graduate of Yale University and Harvard Business School, Zibby currently lives in New York with her four children ages ten to eighteen and her husband Kyle Owens, co-president and founder of Morning Moon Productions. Follow her on Instagram @ZibbyOwens and Substack where she tells it like it is.

Skylar Liberty Rose is a writer, coach, and pro-aging advocate helping women embrace their forties and fifties with passion and purpose. Through courses, coaching, and circles, she offers midlife women an opportunity to move past ageist stereotypes, challenge a culture of anti-aging, and create meaningful change in their lives. Born in London, Skylar moved to New York City when she was forty. Her work has been highlighted by numerous high-profile publications, and her 2020 documentary diary, *A Woman in the World*, is featured in the US National Women's History Museum. Visit her website at SkylarLibertyRose.com.

Tonya Parker is a writer, blogger, and social media influencer. She was a brand ambassador for *The Oprah Magazine* for over five years and won the magazine's first Partner Award in 2017. She has been featured in *The Oprah Magazine*, *Upscale*, *Business Insider*, and *Essence* and has been cast in several nationally syndicated commercials. In addition to her career as a blogger and influencer, Tonya holds a master's degree in education and is a licensed school counselor. She is currently working on her debut novel.

Rachel Solomon is an author, writer, and Creative Director/Founder of Honor Code Creative, a marketing/branding agency grounded in powerful emotional storytelling. Formerly the fashion/beauty editor of *BostonNow* and stuffy columnist for *Stuff Magazine*, her work has been published in *The Harvard AIDS Review*, *The Boston Globe*, and *InStyle*, among others. She is the winner of *The Improper Bostonian*'s short story prize, and her fiction has appeared in all three *Fenway Fiction* anthologies. Her novel *Number Six Fumbles* was published by Simon & Schuster/MTV Books, and her piece "The End of an Era" from *The Pennsylvania Gazette* was optioned as a screenplay. As "Hey Mrs. Solomon," Rachel writes a widely read Substack newsletter about style for women over forty (she calls this time period "arriving"), publishes a style diary on Instagram @HeyMrsSolomon, and advises women on finding their style DNA at HeyMrsSolomon. com. She lives in Miami with her husband, three cats, and a guest room turned closet. They have a beloved son who lives in New England, where they spend summers.

Susan Swimmer is the Founder and Creative Director of jewelry brand Evie Marques. A former writer, magazine editor, and TV correspondent, Susan was the deputy editor of *Cosmopolitan* magazine, the fashion features director of *More* magazine, the features editor-at-large at *Marie Claire* magazine, and the special projects editor of *Seventeen* magazine. Her work has been published in *Glamour, Elle, Marie Claire UK, Mirabella, Manhattan, The Purist, Condé Nast Traveler*, and *Biography*, among others. Swimmer's interviews have included world leaders (President Bill Clinton), celebrities (Brooke Shields, Drew Barrymore, Gwyneth Paltrow, Gwen Stefani), athletes (Kristi Yamaguchi, Andre Agassi, Lance Armstrong), designers (Donna Karan, Carolina Herrera, Vera Wang, Isaac Mizrahi, Tory Burch), icons (Farrah Fawcett, Joan Rivers, Lauren Hutton), and real people who do extraordinary things (a woman with a massive rare book collection, a master frame carver). Considered an expert on style and pop culture, Swimmer has appeared on the *Today* show, *The Oprah Winfrey Show, Good Morning America, Entertainment Tonight, E!*, and CNN's *Showbiz Today*, and she has been interviewed by *The New York Times, The Los Angeles Times, USA Today*, and local newspapers nationwide. Swimmer is the author of two books, *Michelle Obama: First Lady of Fashion and Style* (Blackdog & Leventhal, June 2009) and *Is He The One? 101 Questions That Will Lead You To The Truth* (Andrews McMeel, 2004). Susan lives in New York City. She can be found at EvieMarques.com.

Natalie Y. Wester is a radical reinventor, permission-giver, and storyteller, encouraging midlife women to give themselves permission to change the life they're living so they can live a life they love. Natalie is a former second-grade teacher who once stood in the Oval Office with the president of the United States as a National State Teacher of the Year. Before becoming a teacher, she worked in business for more than twenty years, including as a company vice president and the owner of an award-winning consulting practice. In 2019, Natalie retired at the age of fifty-nine. She has spent the last five years reimagining midlife as a first-time solo traveler who wandered around the world for seventy days, an over-sixty whiskey distillery intern who made bourbon, an award-winning writer, a solo expat currently living in Portugal, a blogger, and a latitude 66 S explorer when she crosses the Antarctic Circle on an expedition to Antarctica for her sixty-fifth birthday.

Laura Friedman Williams is the author of *Available: A Very Honest Account of Life After Divorce*, which explores themes of self-discovery, resilience, and the complexities of relationships. She is a frequent contributor of personal essays to *Human Parts* on *Medium*, where she has continued to blend personal reflection with themes of family, love, sex, loss, and the pursuit of fulfillment. She has also written for *Vogue UK*, has been featured in *The New York Post*, and has appeared on dozens of podcasts discussing midlife divorce. She lives in New York City.

About the Authors

Dina Alvarez started her writing career as a freelancer for *Big Apple Parent* in New York City covering education, local politics, and lifestyle. She later co-founded *SomosPadres*, the first and only bilingual parenting publication for Hispanic families in New York City. Dina continues to write in her spare time with a focus on creative nonfiction pieces. She is an avid reader and lover of anthologies, particularly those that tell women's stories. Dina is the mother of two adult sons and a native New Yorker. She continues to call the city home where she lives with her husband.

Dina Aronson is passionate about shining a light on midlife women and reframing the cultural conversation around aging. She began her career as an attorney, later founding a legal search firm, but pivoted as she approached midlife and couldn't find relevant content that reflected her experience. She began freelancing for start-ups aimed at the forty-plus woman, and founded the *Patina* blog, now a Substack newsletter called *Patina with Dina Aronson*, where she explores topics in and around aging through her midlife lens. She has two grown stepsons, and currently resides between New York City and Miami with her husband.